Volker Flögel

The Microstructure of European Bond Markets

WIRTSCHAFTSWISSENSCHAFT

ebs **Forschung**

Schriftenreihe der
EUROPEAN BUSINESS SCHOOL
International University Schloß Reichartshausen

Herausgegeben von
Univ.-Prof. Dr. Utz Schäffer

Band 60

Die EUROPEAN BUSINESS SCHOOL (ebs) – gegründet im Jahr 1971 – ist Deutschlands älteste private Wissenschaftliche Hochschule für Betriebswirtschaftslehre im Universitätsrang. Dieser Vorreiterrolle fühlen sich ihre Professoren und Doktoranden in Forschung und Lehre verpflichtet. Mit der Schriftenreihe präsentiert die EUROPEAN BUSINESS SCHOOL (ebs) ausgewählte Ergebnisse ihrer betriebs- und volkswirtschaftlichen Forschung.

Volker Flögel

The Microstructure of European Bond Markets

Organization, Price Formation, and Cost of Liquidity

With a foreword by Prof. Dr. Lutz Johanning

Deutscher Universitäts-Verlag

Bibliografische Information Der Deutschen Bibliothek
Die Deutsche Bibliothek verzeichnet diese Publikation in der Deutschen Nationalbibliografie; detaillierte bibliografische Daten sind im Internet über <http://dnb.ddb.de> abrufbar.

Dissertation European Business School Oestrich-Winkel, 2006

D 1540

1. Auflage August 2006

Lektorat: Ute Wrasmann / Britta Göhrisch-Radmacher

Der Deutsche Universitäts-Verlag ist ein Unternehmen von Springer Science+Business Media.
www.duv.de

Umschlaggestaltung: Regine Zimmer, Dipl.-Designerin, Frankfurt/Main
Druck und Buchbinder: Rosch-Buch, Scheßlitz
Gedruckt auf säurefreiem und chlorfrei gebleichtem Papier
Printed in Germany

ISBN-10 3-8350-0423-9
ISBN-13 978-3-8350-0423-8

Foreword

The volumes outstanding in bond markets are by far larger than in equity markets. Despite this fact, most of the research on the microstructure of financial markets focuses on equity markets. This is even more surprising taking into account that (i) the microstructure of a financial market has a strong influence on its ability to allocate resources efficiently, and (ii) that the results obtained from equity markets cannot be applied to bond markets. The thesis addresses open questions related to the microstructure of bond markets and presents three empirical studies.

In the first paper, a unique dataset of transactions in German federal securities is analyzed to address the question whether the historical grown structure of different coexisting trading segments – exchange trading, bilateral OTC trading, and brokered OTC trading – can be economically justified. There is evidence that the different trading segments are indeed regarded as non-interchangeable by the market participants.

The second part of the thesis focuses on the price formation in customer-dealer and the interdealer bond markets by applying cointegration econometrics to a dataset of high frequency quotes for EMU government bonds. While the customer-dealer market is still very fragmented and intransparent, trading in the interdealer market concentrates on a smaller number of more transparent electronic trading systems like EuroMTS. There is evidence that the share of these two markets in the price formation process depends strongly on the liquidity of a bond. For very liquid bonds the customer-dealer market is dominant, but its information share is much lower for less liquid bonds. This result shows that the prevailing structure in bond markets is especially suited for less liquid bonds.

In the last paper the author concentrates on the cost of liquidity of euro denominated investment grade corporate bonds. This is of particular interest regarding the current efforts of the NASD to make US corporate bond markets more transparent. Surprisingly, the smaller size of the euro bond market and the lack of transparency do not translate into higher cost of liquidity.

Overall, Volker Flögel can generate new results which should be of considerable interest to bond market participants, regulators, and financial researchers.

Professor Dr. Lutz Johanning

Acknowledgements

This thesis is the result of my work as a research assistant and doctoral student at the Endowed Chair for Asset Management at the EUROPEAN BUSINESS SCHOOL, International University Schloß Reichartshausen, between September 2002 and March 2006. During this time, I had the privilege of co-operating with a number of people to whom I would like to express my warmest gratitude.

First of all, I would like to thank my supervisor, Prof. Dr. Lutz Johanning, who made this research project possible and provided ongoing support during my time as a research assistant and doctoral student at his chair. I also thank Prof. Dr. Dirk Schiereck, my second supervisor, for many helpful discussions and comments.

My special thanks go to Dr. Christoph Kesy for being a great friend and an inspiring co-author whose constant encouragement animated me to embark on a doctoral thesis. His knowledge on bond markets contributed a lot to the research on hand. Furthermore, I am grateful to Anja Hechenblaikner for reading some of my papers and for her advice, beyond research.

Over the years, I have become indebted to many people at the EUROPEAN BUSINESS SCHOOL for their suggestions and comments. I owe many thanks to Timo Geken in particular for introducing me to the field of "Merger Waves", and to my other colleagues at the Endowed Chair for Asset Management and the Endowed Chair for Banking and Finance, namely Martin Ahnefeld, Christian Funke, Carolin Fuß, Philipp Henrich, Jana Kitzmann, Benjamin Kleidt, Markus Mentz, Gaston Michel, Christoph Sigl-Grüb, Trudel Thullen, Christian Voigt, and Sebastian Werner.

Additionally, I would like to express my warmest gratitude to Venky Panchapagesan, who gave me the opportunity to spend unforgettable months at John M. Olin School of Business at Washington University in St. Louis, where most of the work was done on the last part of the thesis. I thank the German Academic Exchange Service for the financial support during my time in St. Louis.

I would also like to thank my family, who were an important source of support during this research and during my preceding studies at the University of Munich. They enabled me to establish a balance between everyday life and research life. Finally, I thank Isabell Kober for her support and patience and for the unforgettable time in addition to university life.

Volker Flögel

Contents

List of Figures

List of Tables

1 Introduction

1.1 Motivation

Financial markets have the important role to aggregate and allocate resources and risks in time and space. In order to do design markets that fulfill this role as efficient as possible, it is important to know how financial markets are organized, how they are regulated, how trades are executed and paid for, and finally, what impact these issues have on the price formation. These questions are extensively treated in a field of research called market microstructure.

While the different facets of the market microstructure theory are well exploited for the stock market,[1] research on bond markets just arose in recent years.[2] This is surprising considering the importance of bond markets. The ECB (European Central Bank) reported that euro area investment funds have total assets of euro 1,179.4 billion in bond funds but only euro 797.1 billion in equity funds.[3] However, research on the microstructure of bond markets is limited due to the decentralized and opaque nature of these markets and, therefore, poor data availability.

Because of the differences between bond and equity markets, theoretical as well as empirical results from equity markets cannot necessarily be transferred. This dissertation is motivated by these differences. Therefore, the most important aspects are reviewed in the next paragraphs.[4]

The first difference is the definition of private information in both markets. In equity markets, private information is defined as superior information on an asset's (future) value. Prices of government securities and, to a large extent, prices of investment grade corporate bonds are strongly dependant on the term structure of the underlying risk-free interest rates,[5] which in turn, depend on macroeconomic factors that are made publicly available at the same time to all investors through electronic information systems. Therefore, private information on a bond's fundamental value is

---

1 For an overview see O'Hara (1995), Madhavan (2000), .Biais, Glosten, and Spatt (2004).
2 See, e.g., Gravelle (2002) for bond markets and Lyons (2001) for FX (foreign exchange) markets.
3 See European Central Bank (2005), p. 25 of the euro area statistics money, banking and investment funds.
4 The categorization follows Gravelle (2002). Although he focuses on government securities markets, most of his arguments also apply to corporate bonds with investment grade rating.
5 See Schultz (2001), pp. 682-683.

very unlikely to occur in these markets and, as a result, traditional asymmetric information models like Kyle (1985) are ill-suited to describe the trading process in bond markets. However, it is very likely that dealers in bond markets have private information on the state of the trading environment such as customer order flow. This payoff irrelevant private information is an important determinant of the price discovery process in multiple dealership markets.[6]

Besides the differences in the definition of private information, bonds differ from stocks in other characteristics as well. One distinctive feature is the finite maturity of bonds that leads to a change in the bond's liquidity and yield dynamics during its lifetime. With increasing age of a bond, buy and hold investors absorb a large fraction of the issue in their portfolios and, therefore, reduce the floating supply available for trading.[7] Another distinctive feature is that the homogeneity among bonds is much larger than among equities. This results in a larger co-movement in terms of yield dynamics and, in turn, implies a greater ease of inventory price hedging in bond markets relative to equity markets. Since two-thirds to three-fourths of the price variation in investment grade corporate bonds can be explained by variations in government securities,[8] a dealer can even hedge the risk associated with holding an unwanted inventory in these bonds to a large extent by trading government securities or futures on government securities.

Structural differences between bond and equity dealership markets exist regarding the low degree of centralization of bond markets. Overall, three features associated with the bond markets' low degree of centralization cannot be modeled by specialist-based single-dealer theories applied to equity markets such as NYSE (New York Stock Exchange). First, the competition for customer order flow among dealers. Second, the existence of two trading environments: a public environment (the customer-dealer market), where customers trade exclusively with dealers, and an interdealer environment (the interdealer market), where liquidity providers trade among themselves. The third feature refers to the further fragmentation of these two trading environments into several trading segments (exchange, OTC bilateral, and brokered OTC).

---

6 See Lyons (2001), pp. 63-112 and Rapporport (1999), p. 143.
7 See Amihud and Mendelson (1991), p. 1413.
8 See Schultz (2001), pp. 682-683.

Finally, equity and bond markets also differ in transparency. The transparency of a market is related to its degree of centralization and refers to the amount of information (pre- and post-trade) available to the public. Multiple-dealer equity markets such as NASDAQ (National Association of Securities Dealers Automated Quotations) or LSE (London Stock Exchange) are linked electronically and are thus more centralized than multiple-dealer bond markets. Customers have access to the best bid- and ask-quote and can also trade a predetermined volume at these quotes. Additionally, information on completed trades is published to the public in these markets. In bond markets, quotes are not firm, tradeable volume is rarely posted, and post trade information is usually not published.[9]

The existing differences between multiple-dealer bond and multiple-dealer equity markets are large and point out why an application of the results from equity markets to bond markets is not necessarily possible. Of course, the dissertation cannot cover all distinctive features of the microstructure of bond markets, but the results allow some new and interesting insights into bond markets and multiple-dealer markets in general. The next section gives an overview on the facets of the microstructure of bond markets that are covered in the dissertation and its organization.

1.2 Overview and Organization

The objective of the dissertation is to shed some further light on the microstructure of bond markets. A natural starting point is the organizational structure. As noted above, different trading segments coexist in bond markets: exchange trading, bilateral OTC trading, and brokered OTC trading. Part 2 analyzes for the first time the historically grown organizational structure of the customer-dealer as well as the interdealer market for government bonds and examines whether these structures are economically justified. Based on transaction-cost-theoretical considerations, hypotheses are derived on the relationship between the specificity of a transaction and the market participants' trading segment choice. These hypotheses are empirically tested with a unique dataset

---

9 Exceptions are some electronic customer-dealer trading systems. Information on completed trades is published to the systems' participants, but still no to the broad public. Another exception is the exchange trading, but trading volume in this trading segment is too small to be relevant for institutional investors. The data of institutional trades used in Part 4, e.g., contains only OTC trades and no exchange trades.

comprising more than 180,000 trades in 52 German federal securities provided by the Federal Supervisory Office for Securities Trading (Bundesaufsichtsamt für Wertpapierwesen, BAWe), today Federal Financial Supervisory Authority (Bundesanstalt für Finanzdienstleistungsaufsicht, BAFin). The analysis shows that the existing parallel trading possibilities are actually regarded as non-interchangeable by the market participants. The choice of the trading segment depends on security as well as order characteristics, especially order size. In summary, our analysis shows that the prevailing structure of the secondary market for German federal securities with several differently organized trading segments is economically justified. Each segment of the secondary market for German federal securities satisfies different transaction needs.

Following O'Hara (2003), financial markets provide price formation and liquidity.[10] These are the two microstructure issues addressed in Part 3 and Part 4 of the thesis. Part 3 analyzes the short-run dynamics and relationship between the customer-dealer and the interdealer market. The sample covers euro government bonds issued by members of the EMU (European Monetary Union). During the observation periods, all bonds were traded on EuroMTS, an electronic interdealer system for euro benchmark government bonds. The focus of Part 3 is to reveal each market's contribution to the price discovery process of these bonds. In contradiction to the commonly held belief that the interdealer market slightly leads the customer-dealer market,[11] the empirical results provide evidence that the customer-dealer market dominates the price discovery process for euro benchmark government bonds. However, the contribution of the interdealer market to the price discovery depends on bond characteristics. The share in the price discovery process of the interdealer market is larger for less liquid bonds than for liquid bonds.

Part 4 of the dissertation examines the cost of liquidity in the customer-dealer market for euro corporate bonds. There is recent indication that bond trading costs have gone down considerably since the US markets became more transparent with the introduction of TRACE (Trade Reporting and Compliance Engine) by the NASD (National Association of Securities Dealers). Euro bond markets, unlike the US, are still largely opaque and post-trade information is largely absent. In addition, these markets are considerably smaller in size compared to the US, but have been growing rapidly

10 See O'Hara (2003), p. 1338.
11 See, e.g., Lyons (2001), p. 115.

since the introduction of the euro. Empirical evidence is presented for the first time that this lack of transparency and smaller market size do not, however, translate into greater trading costs, at least for large institutional investors. Unlike other studies that impute trading costs from trade prices alone, we are able to measure these costs directly using quotations from multiple dealers prior to the trade. Moreover, we present results that suggest that trading costs in bond markets are sensitive to market conditions prior to the trade, as in equity markets. We contrast costs of trading similar sizes in equity and bonds of the same issuers and find that bonds cost roughly a little less than 10% of the cost of trading equity.

Finally, Part 5 summarizes the results and gives an overview on possible directions for further research on the microstructure of bond markets.

The thesis is presented as a collection of research papers. As a consequence, the notation may differ per chapter and some definitions as well as aspects of the organizational structure of bond markets may be repetitive. A German version of Part 2 of this dissertation has already been published as Floegel and Kesy (2004) in Kredit und Kapital. Part 4 is based on a working paper published as Floegel, Kesy, and Panchapagesan (2005).

2 The Organizational Structure of the Secondary Market for Federal Securities: Historically grown! Economically justified?

2.1 Introduction

The secondary market for federal securities is the economically most important and the most liquid spot market segment of European securities markets. In Germany, the organization of federal securities trading in the secondary market has evolved historically through parallel on- and off-exchange (over the counter, OTC) structures. Generally, three differently structured trading possibilities for federal securities can be identified:

- Exchange trading
- Bilateral OTC trading
- Brokered OTC trading.

The majority of transactions are conducted bilateral OTC. These trades are negotiated directly between institutional counterparties. Nevertheless, exchanges and independent brokers are also able to account for a significant proportion of the turnover in the secondary market for German federal securities. This article examines for the first time whether these economically distinct trading segments fulfill unique investor needs and, therefore, whether their existence is economically justified.

Contrary to equities, price formation in the spot market for federal securities does not result from meeting supply and demand at one central secondary market. The actual valuation procedure takes place on the basis of yield curves, which are provided to market participants through the well known electronic information systems like Bloomberg or Reuters in real time. If however the quality of the price discovery can be excluded to a large extent as a criterion for the market participants' choice of the trading possibility, then the operational efficiency of the trading segment, i.e. in particular the costs of the order execution, is the deciding factor of the trading segment choice.[12]

[12] See Nabben and Rudolph (1994), p. 172.

At the beginning, we therefore consider neoinstitutional transaction cost theory, which examines the institutional arrangement of transaction conditions that cannot be coordinated frictionless over markets because of information asymmetry and transaction costs.[13] Before defining the background of our problem, the different trading segments themselves are to be understood as institutions.[14] In the context of the analysis we assume the minimization of transaction costs as a whole to be the dominant factor in the decision criterion for the trading segment choice of market participants. According to the transaction costs approach, we identify contractor search costs, control costs due to price risks as well as settlement costs as the crucial cost components of the trading segment choice of investors in federal securities trading. Different developments of these costs for the three trading segments result from the interaction of the trading mechanism with the degree of specificity of a transaction desire. The existence of each individual "market place" is economically justified if it represents the most efficient trading mechanism for the market participants under total cost criteria for at least one certain type of transaction. Following on from this is an empirical examination of how individual decisions of market participants for a certain trading segment are systematically related to the degree of transaction specificity. If this relationship is not confirmed, then this would point to the fact that manifested institutional conditions predominantly maintained historically grown, but not economically justified market structures.

Section 2.2 classifies the present analysis into the context of the existing scientific literature. Subsequently, Section 2.3 presents the organizational structures dominant in the market for German federal securities and the fundamental decision situation of market participants concerning trading segment choice. In Section 2.4 the hypotheses on the decision behavior of market participants are derived, describing in particular, why the degree of transaction specificity plays an important role for the trading segment choice in the government securities market. The dataset used to test the hypotheses is presented in Section 2.5. This concerns a unique dataset for the biannual period from January through June 2001. Altogether the data comprise 189.129 exchange and OTC transactions in 52 different federal securities with fixed coupon. Sections 2.6 and 2.7 empirically examine the determinants of the choice of the trading segment. For

---

13 See Schmidt and Terberger (1997), p. 396 and p. 399, as well as Coase (1937) and Williamson (1975) for the transaction cost approach.

14 See Krahnen (1993), p. 803.

this purpose, the probabilities for the choice of the different trading segments are modeled using logistic and multinomial logistic regressions. Besides the most important variable, order size, additional explanatory variables like issued amount, time to maturity, coupon, and deliverability (into a Eurex futures contract) are included in the econometric model. Finally, the results are summarized in Section 2.8. The results also allow an outlook on the future development of the organizational structures in the secondary market for German federal securities.

2.2 Theoretical Background

Extremely rich stock dealing literature is available which investigates important individual components of the microstructure of secondary markets. Mentioned here are the numerous empirical investigations of the pros and cons of computer and floor trading systems,[15] the adverse price effects of large trading volumes[16] as well as experimental investigations of the degree of secondary market transparency[17] and the privileges of stockbrokers and market makers.[18] Apart from this rich analysis of individual aspects of the microstructure of secondary markets within the context of microstructure-theoretical research, attention is also dedicated to the phenomenon of the coexistence of several trading segments in equity markets. Here, extensive model-theoretical and experimental research work illustrates that, due to purely information-economic considerations, a stable market equilibrium with more than one trading segment can exist.[19] The explanatory approaches are based on the basic assumption of an asymmetrical information distribution regarding the future asset value with the result that uninformed dealers at secondary markets prefer the greatest possible transparency and nonanonymity of counterparties, whereas informed market participants prefer trading mechanisms that protect the value of fundamental private information. A transaction-cost-based explanation provides the theoretical investigations of Pagano (1989) and Viswanathan and Wang (2002). Although transaction-cost-theoretical explanations do not exclude an asymmetrical information distribution

15 See, e.g., Cohen et al. (1986), Grünbichler (1994), Franke and Hess (1998), Theissen (2002).
16 See, e.g., Holthausen, Leftwich, and Mayers (1987), Holthausen, Leftwich, and Mayers (1990).
17 See, e.g., Flood et al. (1999), Bloomfield and O'Hara (2000).
18 See, e.g., Gerke, Arneth, and Bosch (2000), Gerke, Arneth, and Shya (2000).
19 See, e.g., Easley and O'Hara (1987), Seppi (1990), Madhavan (1995), Easley, Kiefer, and O'Hara (1996), Subrahmanyam (1997), Naik, Neuberger, and Viswanathan (1999), and Bloomfield and O'Hara (2000).

between market participants, it does not stand in the foreground.[20] Viswanathan and Wang (2002) examine why numerous secondary equity markets could develop a hybrid organizational structure, integrating both limit order book and dealership market structure. Viswanathan and Wang (2002) conclude that, due to transaction cost considerations, a bundling of "smaller" orders within a limit order book and "larger" orders in the dealership market is explainable. Pagano (1989) also confirms that a stable market equilibrium, in that small and large order volumes are executed in different market segments, can mint itself purely from cost considerations. For large transactions, he also explicitly includes the possibility of bilateral, with search costs connected OTC-trading into his theoretical analysis.[21]

Stenzel (1995) empirically examines the causes of off-exchange trading in German equities. He explains the existence of a parallel off-exchange trading environment with the factors transaction costs, liquidity, market participant structure, quality of settlement and market transparency. Schiereck (1995) studies the stock exchange choice of institutional investors for the trading of internationally listed German companies. He determines i.a. transaction costs, liquidity, settlement quality, market efficiency, insider protection, and market transparency as important decision factors. The results of Stenzel (1995) and Schiereck (1995) document the importance of transaction costs to the parallel existence of several trading segments. Apart from the explicit costs, the term "transaction costs" specifically subsumes the hidden implicit transaction costs which are particularly expressed through liquidity, transparency, and insider protection. The investigation of Picot, Bortenlänger, and Röhrl (1996) provides stringent transaction-cost-theoretical systematics for the explanation of the structure of secondary market trading in equities. The authors divide the transaction costs phase-oriented into contact, contract, control and adjustment costs and evaluate the individual kinds of costs verbal-analytically for different trading segments. Fong, Madhavan, and Swan (2001) use transaction data to analyze the market segment choice of market participants in the Australian equity market. They determine the liquidity in the downstairs market and the order volume as the most important influencing factors of the decision for the order-driven downstairs trade segment or the broker-dealer-segment (upstairs-segment). None of the results of the work of Stenzel (1995), Schiereck (1995),

---

20 See Schmidt and Terberger (1997), p. 398.

21 See Pagano (1989), pp. 268-269 and Viswanathan and Wang (2002), pp. 152-153.

Picot, Bortenlänger, and Röhrl (1996), and Fong, Madhavan, and Swan (2001) generally stand in contradiction to the purely information-economic approach, since the degree of asymmetric information distribution at the market is reflected in the total costs of trading.[22]

In contrast to equity markets, no results from similar studies of the microstructure of the market for federal securities exist. To our knowledge, there are also no investigations of the international bond markets that can be consulted as a basis for an explanation of the organizational structure of the secondary market for German federal securities. Furthermore, it can be assumed that the well accepted information-economic explanation for equity markets cannot be transferred in this form to the secondary market for federal securities, since private fundamental information has no relevance in the trading of government securities.[23] Hence, an economic explanation of the individual trading segments must be particularly based on transaction-cost-theoretical considerations.

2.3 Organizational Structure of the Secondary Market for Federal Securities

Federal securities are traded at German exchanges as well as OTC. The daily exchange trading of German federal securities concentrates on the stock exchanges in Frankfurt, Stuttgart, Munich, Duesseldorf, Berlin, Bremen, Hanover and Hamburg. The floor trading at German exchanges is organized as an auction market, which bundles the transaction requests of the market participants. The transmission of the orders to the order book of an exchange floor normally takes place via the stock exchange members through an automatic order routing system.[24] Non-stock exchange members (e.g. private customers) hand their orders over to a stock exchange member, who feeds the transaction requests in the order book in exchange for the payment of a commission fee. The specialist (amtlicher Kursmakler) fixes the official price on the basis of all available orders in the order book.

---

22 See Schiereck (1995), pp. 79-171, Stenzel (1995), pp. 169-194, Picot, Bortenlänger, an Röhrl (1996), pp. 18-19, and Fong, Madhavan, and Swan (2001), p. 35.

23 See Kesy (2003), pp. 4-9 and pp. 23-26, as well as the articles referenced there.

24 Stock exchange members in Germany are in particular credit institutions and independent brokers.

In contrast to the auction-driven exchange trading, the off-exchange trading of federal securities is organized as a decentralized multiple-dealer market. At a multiple-dealer market, special market participants make the execution of orders for the other market participants possible. This intermediary service in the OTC market for German federal securities is provided by the government bond traders of large banks and trading firms, the so-called dealers.[25] With the continuous determination and quotation of bid- and ask-prices as well as the willingness to take market risk, they offer a continuous trading possibility to their customers, the institutional investors. Each dealer holds an inventory to fulfill the unpredictable orders of the investors. Due to the stochastic nature of the customer order flow, the inventory will regularly deviate from a dealer's preferred inventory. A constant liquidity provision to investors, however, can be ensured by offsetting transactions with other dealers to return to the inventory with the preferred risk and liquidity characteristics.

As a result, the OTC market for federal securities is characterized by two different market spheres: the interdealer sphere and the customer-dealer sphere.[26] In the customer-dealer market, institutional investors (customers) from inland and abroad – insurance companies, asset managers, pension funds, industrial enterprises, smaller banks, smaller central banks and hedge funds – trade always directly and nonanonymously with the liquidity providing dealers. In the interdealer market the liquidity providers trade exclusively among themselves. In contrast to the customer-dealer market, dealers have the possibility to use the anonymous service of an independent broker. Brokers are pure matchmakers bringing dealers anonymously together in exchange for a small fee. Besides the nondisclosure of the dealer's identity, the broker also searches the counterparty for the dealer. Figure 2.1 illustrates the market spheres of the OTC market for federal securities.

---

25 In principle, dealers and market makers can be active in a multiple-dealer market. The separation criterion between a dealer and a market maker is in practice that a dealer does not have an obligation to offer liquidity at the market. A dealer places indicative bid-and ask-quotes, which signal a price indication to the market participants. That differentiates a dealer in the government bond market of a market maker in the Jumbo Pfandbrief market. The market maker places obligatory and tradeable bid- and ask-quotes up to a certain maximum volume.

26 See Gravelle (2002), p. 7.

Figure 2.1: Market Spheres of the OTC Spot Market[27]

This figure shows the different market spheres in the off-exchange market. The outer ring represents the customer-dealer market (public sphere) and the inner ring represents the interdealer trading environment (interdealer sphere). The OTC interdealer sphere again consists of two segments, the direct or bilateral trading and the brokered interdealer trading.

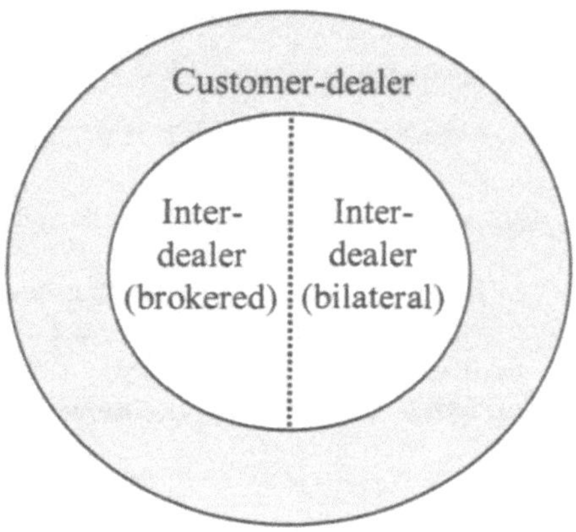

For decades the entire OTC market for bonds was a pure telephone market.[28] Different electronic trading systems in the customer-dealer market and in the interdealer market, which could already accommodate an important portion of the entire order flow in federal bonds, have only existed for a few years.[29] However, the question of communication medium and/or degree of automation of different trading platforms can be neglected for our trading segment decision analysis, since the traditional characteristics regarding anonymity and price formation were taken over for the OTC market (customer-dealer and interdealer) as well as brokered interdealer market: (a) The established electronic trading systems are fed continuously with the bid- and ask-quotes of the dealer and, thus, replicate the traditional organizational form of the multiple-dealer market. (b) Beyond that, the anonymity of the counterparties up to the

27 The representation of the market spheres of the OTC market for federal securities follows the representation of the market spheres of the foreign-exchange market in Lyons (2001), p. 43.

28 See Stucki (2000), p. 333.

29 For a complete overview of the development of the world-wide electronic bond trading and a detailed representation of all existing trading platforms, see The Bond Market Association (2002).

execution is protected in the electronic systems of independent brokers, whereas in the trading systems operated by dealers, the anonymity of the contractors was not given during the investigation period.[30]

Figure 2.2 exhibits the different trading segments in the interdealer as well as the customer-dealer market. The institutional investors in the customer-dealer market have access to two different trading segments. Transactions can be executed either at the exchange or in the bilateral OTC market with a liquidity provider as counterparty. The decision situation in the interdealer market is extended by a third alternative. Liquidity providers can also make use of the service of a broker in the OTC market.

Figure 2.2: Decision Situation in the Customer-Dealer and Interdealer Market

This figure exhibits the decision situation in the customer-dealer and the interdealer market. Market participants in the interdealer sphere have the choice between exchange trading, bilateral OTC trading and brokered OTC trading. Investors in the customer-dealer market can either trade at the exchange or OTC bilateral with a liquidity provider (dealer).

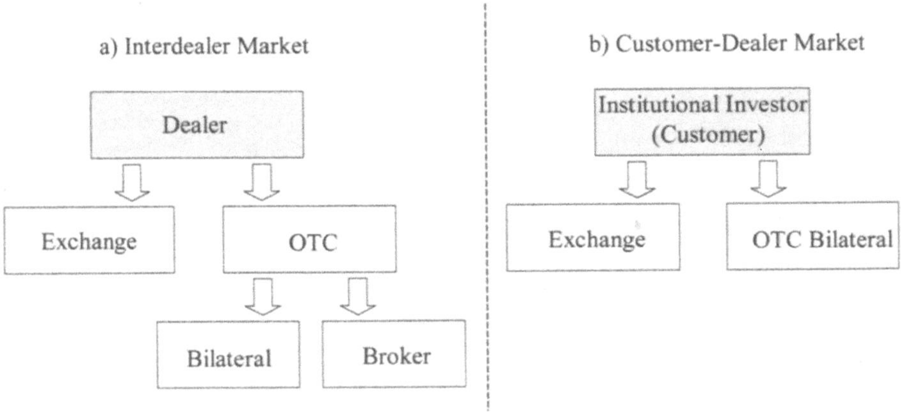

[30] Meanwhile there are the first trading systems, which make an anonymous bilateral trade possible over a central counterpart in the interdealer market. The consequences for future organizational structures of the secondary market for German federal securities will be discussed in Section 2.8 of this article.

2.4 Hypotheses

This section derives hypotheses on the market participants' trading segment decision for both market spheres based on transaction-cost-theoretical considerations. Against the background of the transaction cost theory, a transaction is the exchange of property rights.[31] The costs incurred during the transmission of property rights are called transaction costs.[32] Since these transaction costs reduce the utility of the exchange of property rights, individually rational market participants are anxious to minimize them.

The level of the total costs of a transaction in the secondary market for federal securities depends in particular on two transaction-describing characteristics: uncertainty and specificity. The term uncertainty refers thereby to a characteristic of the federal security itself. The market for government securities is typically characterized by an extremely high uncertainty. Due to regularly arriving new public information, the yield curve relevant for the bond valuation changes continuously and, thus, leads to a new consensus market estimate of the fair value of a federal security. Specificity however reflects the characteristic of a certain transaction desire. In the secondary market for federal securities the term specificity can be replaced to a large extent by the term liquidity requirement, because the most important determinant of specificity is the size of a transaction. With rising order size it becomes increasingly more difficult to find a transaction partner who can make the necessary liquidity available (money or securities) and is at the same time willing to offer a fair price. Due to the regularly very large transaction volumes of institutional market participants, the average transaction specificity is very high in the market for federal securities.[33] In addition, for bond-specific factors, like amount issued, coupon level, time to maturity and deliverability of a federal security into a Eurex futures contract, an influence on the specificity of an order cannot be excluded.[34] The higher the issued amount of the traded bond, the smaller should be the specificity of a transaction in this bond (keeping all

[31] See Commons (1931), p. 652 and Williamson (1990), p. 26.

[32] See, e.g., Williamson (1990), p. 21 and Milgrom and Roberts (1992), p. 29.

[33] 44% of all trades in our sample exhibit a nominal trading volume of more than euro 5 million, 22% of the transactions are as large as euro 10 million and still 8% of the orders are larger than euro 20 million. We cannot observe that individual market participants executed several transactions within short time intervals in identical bond issues. Therefore, it can be concluded that splitting one large order up into several smaller orders is not common practice in federal securities markets - at least during the observation period.

[34] This analysis abstracts by the potential influence of market-related variables like volatility on the specificity of a transaction desire.

other factors constant), since more liquidity is at the disposal of all secondary market activities. A positive effect on the transaction specificity might likewise be attributed to the coupon. Since the data was collected in a period with relatively low interest levels, it can be assumed that higher coupon loans were issued a longer time ago and, therefore, are absorbed to a larger portion in the portfolios of the institutional investors. For the time to maturity, the effect on specificity is not clear. On the one hand bonds that mature later react more strongly to interest rate changes, whereby the search for a counterparty who takes over the price risk for a (large) transaction, is made more difficult. On the other hand, extremely liquid derivative instruments (Bobl and Bund futures) exist for bonds with a time to maturity of 4.5 to 10.5 years that can be used to hedge the price risk almost completely. Also regarding the deliverability of a bond into a Eurex futures contract, the effect on specificity is not clear. It can be regularly observed in the secondary market that the deliverability of a bond leads to a clearly increased trading activity in this issue. To that extent a transaction in a nondeliverable bond is less specific in comparison with a transaction in a deliverable bond. On the other hand, transactions in deliverable bonds also generally exhibit a high specificity, since the subject of the transaction desire is usually a certain deliverable issue. However, a broad (at least partially) replaceable universe of similar federal securities is at the traders' disposal for transaction desires in nondeliverable federal securities.

Transaction costs emerging with bond trading can be divided into search or contact costs, control costs and settlement costs. Search costs are costs which emerge during the initiation of a trade. They are determined predominantly by transaction specificity. Search costs exhibit non-monetary form and monetary form. Non-monetary search costs accrue in particular in the bilateral OTC market in form of the expenditure of counterparty search time. Contrary to equity trading and to brokered OTC trading, a transaction partner must be actively searched, who provides on the one hand the necessary liquidity (money or securities) and, on the other hand, is willing to offer a fair price. The expenditure of time increases with increasing transaction specificity because fewer contractors are potentially able to take the opposite side. Furthermore, with rising specificity, the risk increases that the transaction desire represents information that is processed by the initiator of the trade.[35] This information-economic aspect is based not on private fundamental information on macroeconomic fundamentals, but on the

[35] See Gerke and Rasch (1992), p. 194, and particularly for bond markets Rappoport (2001), p. 143.

knowledge of flows. The knowledge of the identity of a market participant who wants to execute a transaction with high specificity can release imitator behavior[36] or motivate other dealers to opportunistic and unfavorable behavior from the perspective of the initiator of the transaction.[37] From the presented aspects it can be concluded that the counterparty search time for bilateral OTC trades in the secondary market for German federal securities increases with increasing transaction specificity. Monetary search costs arise if the initiator of a transaction does not execute the search for a suitable transaction partner himself. They occur in the interdealer market, as soon as a dealer relies on the services of an independent broker working on a commission basis. Brokers are characterized by a close network of contacts and sources of information, which gives them a good overview on the activities in the intransparent OTC market. Besides, they ensure the anonymity of the transaction initiator, which is favorable under the circumstances explained above. Search costs are the lowest for exchange trades. Usually, a limit order is entered through an electronic order routing system by an exchange member into the central electronic order book.

Control costs occur due to price risks during execution and are justified in the high uncertainty of the transaction relationship. Due to the high absolute exposure to loss, market participants are not willing to enter a large order into an exchange driven limit order book and to wait for the execution of the order.[38] In the auction system of the exchange, an order represents a free trading option for the other market participants whose value increases with the volatility of the market.[39] The value of the free option may be reduced by the initiator of the transaction, by accompanying the order up to

---

36 See Rappoport (2001), p. 143. Lyons (2001), pp. 16-17 describes the relationship between the order flow and exchange rates. Because of the similar structure of FX and fixed income markets, these results presumably also hold for fixed income markets. Additionally, although no private information on macroeconomic fundamentals exist in government bond markets, it can be assumed that market participants form different expectations on the future development of interest rates, or differ in the speed of processing macroeconomic information. Superior forecasts can be the result of more labor resources attributed to internal macroeconomic research. If, in the past, a market participant's order flow was characterized by good forecast ability, the order flow itself is important information that is used by the counterparty to adjust his own expectations.

37 Substantial losses may emerge through a so-called market squeeze. A market squeeze occurs, if, at the secondary market, it becomes generally known by other market participants that certain dealers must buy a high nominal amount in a certain bond to cover a short position or to follow the delivery obligations from derivatives. Potential counterparties could try to use this state of distress to drive up the trade price. Market squeezes in the secondary market for federal securities can lead to a price history for individual federal securities, which is partly uncoupled from the general interest rate level.

38 See Gerke and Rasch (1992), p. 194, and Stoll (1992), p. 85 and p. 88, for an analogous description for equities.

39 See Stoll (1992), p. 82 and p. 85.

execution. In practice that becomes difficult, since each institutional market participant would need an additional trader (at the exchange) who constantly adapts the limit order to the current market conditions. A reduction of price risks associated with exchange trading is, thus, only possible under very high control costs and, since no incentive exists for a market participant to place a limit order with high volume into the order book, institutional market orders are also hardly executable. As a consequence, market participants prefer the off-exchange market for transactions with high specificity due to high nominal order volume. This makes it possible to reduce price risks, and concomitantly control costs, during the execution to zero since the transaction conditions are subject of the negotiation between the counterparties up to mutual agreement. The order is executed instantaneously after the negotiation at the price agreed upon. For small order sizes the problem of the free trading option is to a large extent negligible due to the low absolute exposures to loss.[40] Here, the exchange offers clear advantages regarding the expenditure of counterparty search time through automatic order routing as well as central liquidity bundling. In particular, the transaction desires of the retail customer segment, which are typically characterized by a small order size and are executed by exchange members in exchange for a commission fee, are routed automatically to the exchange.

Settlement costs are costs which arise during the processing of an order, i.e. with the exchange of securities and money. If errors occur during the settlement, then additional adjustment costs emerge from the correction of the settlement procedures. Settlement costs are, to a large extent, independent of transaction specificity and differ depending on the trading segment. It can be assumed that the settlement of exchange transactions generally causes the lowest settlement costs. The EDP (electronic data processing) interfaces between market participants and exchanges have already existed over a long period and the market participants are experienced with the settlement of exchange transactions. In the bilateral OTC market and brokered OTC market, electronic interfaces must be created individually for important market participants and central custodians if necessary. Often, settlement is carried out manually in several steps. Due to a lesser degree of standardization, settlement errors will also occur more frequently in the OTC market than with exchange trades. Thus adjustment costs are also higher for OTC trades than for exchange trades.

---

40 See Stoll (1992), p. 88.

Figure 2.3 shows the relationship between market segment, transaction costs, and the specificity of a trade. With increasing specificity, a trade is first executed at the exchange, then OTC bilateral and finally OTC brokered. Above all, the determining factor whether a market participant trades at the exchange or OTC is the specificity-related variable order volume. Exchange trading is characterized by the smallest search costs and settlement costs. With rising trade volume of a transaction this advantage is overcompensated by higher control costs. As soon as the transaction desire exceeds a certain trade volume, the control costs are so high due to price risks that it is rational for the initiator to exchange the uncertainty connected with the price risk for the higher settlement costs and the higher search costs of a bilateral OTC transaction. Trade volume also considerably affects the decision whether an off-exchange order is executed bilaterally or through a broker. Additionally, it can be expected that bond-related specificity variables also have an impact on the trading segment decision. As soon as the non-monetary search costs of the transaction become too high in the bilateral OTC trading because of increasing specificity of the order, market participants make use of the services of an independent broker. The broker searches the counterparty on behalf of the initiator of the transaction in return for a commission payment. Due to the brokers' knowledge of the order flow, neutrality as intermediary, and ensured anonymity, search costs can turn out to be lower than those of the transaction initiator. With sufficiently high specificity therefore, the commission and settlement costs for a brokered OTC trade can be lower than the total costs for a bilateral OTC trade.

Figure 2.3: Transaction Costs, Specificity, and Trading Segment[41]

This figure drafts the transaction costs in each trading segment dependant on transaction specificity. It is hypothesized that, with increasing specificity of an order, transaction costs are first cheapest at the exchange, then in the bilateral OTC trading and, finally, for orders with highest specificity in the brokered OTC market.

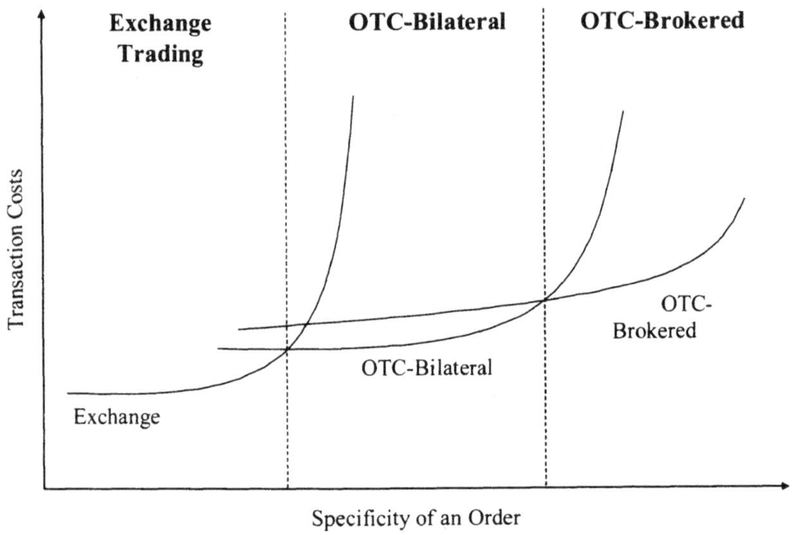

Two hypotheses for the trading segment decision of the market participants result from the transaction-cost-theoretical considerations. While hypothesis H1 is applicable to both, the interdealer market and to the customer-dealer market, hypothesis H2 applies only to the interdealer market since only liquidity providers can make use of the services of an independent broker.

H1: *The higher the order volume, the higher the probability that a transaction will be executed OTC.*

H2: *The higher the transaction specificity of an OTC interdealer trade, the higher the probability that it will be executed through an independent broker.*

41 The representation follows Williamson (1991), p. 284.

In this section, we motivated the crucial systematic influence of transaction specificity on the choice of the trading segment. In the following three sections the systematic relationship formulated in hypotheses H1 and H2 is examined on the basis of a unique dataset.

2.5 Data and Descriptive Statistics

The analysis of the determinants of the trading segment choice is conducted on the basis of a dataset of the former Federal Supervisory Office for Securities Trading (Bundesaufsichtsamt für Wertpapierwesen, BAWe), today Federal Financial Supervisory Authority (Bundesanstalt für Finanzdienstleistungsaufsicht, BAFin).[42] The data altogether covers 189.129 transactions with a nominal value of euro 1.24 billion for the period from January 2001 to June 2001. The trading volume in 52 fixed coupon federal bonds and five-year special federal bonds (Bundesobligationen) refer to an issued volume of euro 508 billion.

By section 9 of the securities trading act (§9 Wertpapierhandelsgesetz, WpHG) in connection with the ordinance on the reporting requirements relating to trades in securities and derivatives (Wertpapierhandel-Meldeverordnung, WpHMV) of the BAFin, market participants are obligated to the daily reporting of completed trades in federal securities to the BAFin. All transactions in securities and derivatives admitted to trading on an organized market in a member state of the European Union or another signatory to the Agreement on the European Economic Area or on the regulated market (Geregelter Markt) or the regulated unofficial market (Freiverkehr) of a German stock exchange are subject to this reporting obligation. At the end of the year 2001, about 5,200 compulsory notifying market participants were registered with the BAWe. Compulsory notifying parties are in principle all domestic credit institutions, financial services institutions as well as foreign credit institutions and enterprises domiciled within Germany.[43] Also independent brokers as well as specialists (Kursmakler) of the exchanges are subject to the obligation of transaction reporting. Apart from the traded nominal amount and the selected market segment (on- or off-exchange), each transaction notification contains, among other things also whether it concerns a

42 We thank the Federal Financial Supervisory Authority (BAFin) for providing the transaction data.
43 See securities trading law section 9, paragraph (1), for the official list of compulsory notifying parties.

customer order or an interdealer order, and, in the case of an interdealer trade, whether an independent broker was involved. Not compulsory notifying parties are the majority of institutional customers of the dealers, as for example, industrial enterprise and insurance companies as well as foreign investors domiciled abroad. The transactions in the 52 Federal bonds should, however, reflect an almost complete picture of the trading in the secondary market for federal securities for the half-yearly observation period. Due to the organizational structure of the market illustrated in Section 2.3, there is at least one notifying party involved in each transaction, except those few trades that are negotiated bilaterally between two counterparties domiciled abroad.

Table 2.1 contains the descriptive statistics of the data. Altogether we observe 98,068 transactions in the customer-dealer market and 91,061 transactions between liquidity providers in the interdealer market. In the observation period 141,024 transactions (74.6% of all transactions) were executed off-exchange. The difference in the on- and off-exchange trading activity becomes even clearer with the statistics for the traded nominal volume, because 94.3% of the nominal volume were traded at the off-exchange secondary market. In the OTC interdealer market, we observe 68,057 transactions that were directly negotiated between the two counterparties, while in the case of 3,342 OTC transactions, an independent broker was assigned the search for the counterparty.

The average transaction volumes in the different trading segments already indicate that the hypotheses derived in Section 2.4 may be confirmed by our results. Trade volume, the most important specificity variable, seems to represent a crucial determinant for the trading segment choice.[44] Nevertheless, this still does not permit a final conclusion on the hypotheses since a variation of the average nominal trading volumes across the different trading segments may also be attributed to security-specific components of transaction specificity: issued amount, time to maturity, coupon and deliverability of a federal bond into a Eurex futures contract. This aspect is considered in the following two sections in the context of the econometric modeling of the probabilities, with which the market participants execute their transactions in different trading segments.

---

[44] The hypothesis of identical average trading volumes in the customer-dealer and the interdealer-market can be rejected on a 1% significance level using parametric as well as nonparametric tests.

Table 2.1: Descriptive Statistics

This table exhibits the descriptive statistic of the transaction data provided by the Federal Financial Supervisory Authority (BAFin) for the half-yearly period from January 2, 2001 until June 29, 2001.

	All Trading Segments	Exchange	OTC	
			Bilateral	Brokered
Overall Market				
No. of Trades	189,129 (100%)	48,105 (25.4%)	137,682 (72.8%)	3,342 (1.8%)
Traded Nominal Volume (million euro)	1,218,843 (100%)	69,715 (5.7%)	1,109,654 (91.0%)	39,473 (3.2%)
Avg. Nominal Volume per Trade (million euro) *(Standard Error)*	6.4 *(0.03)*	1.4 *(0.01)*	8.1 *(0.04)*	11.8 *(0.27)*
Customer-Dealer Market				
No. of Trades	98,068	28,443	69,625	--
Traded Nominal Volume (million euro)	498,448	16,945	481,503	--
Avg. Nominal Volume per Trade (million euro) *(Standard Error)*	5.1 *(0.04)*	0.6 *(0.01)*	6.9 *(0.05)*	-- --
Interdealer Market				
No. of Trades	91,061	19,662	68,057	3,342
Traded Nominal Volume (million euro)	720,395	52,771	628,151	39,473
Avg. Nominal Volume per Trade (million euro) *(Standard Error)*	7.9 *(0.05)*	2.7 *(0.02)*	9.2 *(0.07)*	11.8 *(0.27)*

2.6 Customer-Dealer Market

2.6.1 Empirical Model

Since market participants in the customer-dealer market and in the interdealer market are confronted with different decision situations, the trading segment choice for the two market spheres customer-dealer market and interdealer market is analyzed separately. In the customer-dealer market, institutional investors can either trade at the exchange or OTC bilateral with a dealer. For the analysis of this decision situation and the examination of hypothesis H1 derived in Section 2.4, we estimate a binary logit model of the form

$$(2.1) \qquad \text{Prob}(y = 1 \mid x) = \frac{e^{x'\beta}}{1 + e^{x'\beta}}.$$ [45]

The probability that an investor decides for an off-exchange transaction, $\text{Prob}(y = 1)$, is explained by the specificity variables x. In the prevailing decision situation, the dichotomous variable y takes the value 0, if the investor decides for an exchange transaction and the value 1 if the investor's decision falls in favor of off-exchange trading. The following model is estimated for the customer-dealer market:

$$(2.2) \qquad x'\beta = \beta_0 + \beta_1 \cdot \log(Size) + \beta_2 \cdot AmIss + \beta_3 \cdot Coupon + \beta_4 \cdot TTM + \beta_5 \cdot Deliv\,.$$

Thereby, β_0 is the intercept, log(*Size*) is the logarithm of the order size in terms of nominal value (in million euro)[46], *AmIss* denotes the issued amount of the bond (in billion euro), *Coupon* is the fixed coupon of the bond and *TTM* the time to maturity of the traded bond (in years). *Deliv* labels the deliverability of a bond into a Eurex futures contract and takes the value 1, if the security is deliverable into a Eurex futures contract (Bund, Bobl and Schatz), and 0 otherwise.

---

[45] For a comprehensive representation of logit models, see for example Greene (2003).

[46] Alternative specifications of the model showed that a nonlinear specification of the variable order size substantially improves the fit of the model.

2.6.2 Results and Interpretation

The result of the estimated logit model for the public market sphere is exhibited in Table 2.2. The coefficient estimation confirms the positive influence assumed in hypothesis H1 of the nominal order volume on the probability of the decision to trade at the OTC market. The coefficient is significant at the 1%-level. The bond-related specificity variables have the character of control variables, since they are not explicitly the subject of hypothesis H1. However, most of them are statistically significant, too. The time to maturity and the deliverability of a loan, whose direction of the influence on the transaction specificity could not be clearly derived in Section 2.4, both have a positive impact on the decision for an execution of an order at the OTC market. The coefficients on the time to maturity and the deliverability are significant at the 10%-level and the 1%-level respectively. Also, the regression coefficient of the amount issued has a positive, at the 1%-level significant impact.[47] Altogether the quality of the model with a McFadden-R^2 of over 0.4 is good and the likelihood ratio test rejects the hypothesis that the explanatory variables do not jointly influence the trading segment choice.[48] To test the robustness of the results, the model is estimated separately for the first half and the second half of the observation period. The results are shown in Tables A.2.1 and A.2.2 of the appendix. The regression coefficients on nominal order size, issued amount, and deliverability are indeed very robust. This does not apply to the time to maturity. The coefficient is significant at a 1%-level in both subperiods but with opposite sign.

---

47 The coupon does not have a statistically significant impact on the trading segment decision in the customer-dealer market and was therefore removed from the specification of the final model.

48 See, among others, Backhaus (2003), p. 447.

Table 2.2: Estimation Results for the Customer-Dealer Market

This table exhibits the estimation results from the logit model in Eq. (2.1). The explanatory variables are shown in Eq. (2.2). The variable coupon was omitted from the model estimation since it proved insignificant. The Wald-test is applied to test the statistical significance of the regression coefficients. Respectively, ***, **, and * denote statistical significance at the 1%, 5%, and 10% level.

	$y = 1$ (OTC)
Const	0.918***
log(Size)	0.581***
AmIss	0.061***
TTM	0.002*
Deliv	0.521***
Pseudo-R^2 (McFadden)	0.41
LR-χ^2 (Likelihood Ratio Test)	48,480***
Number of Observations	98,068

In order to draw a final conclusion on the relevance of the statistically significant determinants, a graphical analysis to reveal the economic significance of the explanatory variables is conducted. Therefore, the fitted probability (based on the above specified model), with which an investor in the customer-dealer market decides to trade in the OTC market, is plotted against different values of the explanatory variable of interest. For all other explanatory variables, the arithmetic means are assumed and held constant. Figure 2.4 shows – separately for deliverable and nondeliverable bonds – the fitted probability of an OTC transaction based on the logit model in dependence of different nominal order sizes. Both lines signal an economically significant positive relationship. While the probability for an off-exchange transaction in a nondeliverable bond with a nominal order size of euro 0.1 million is about 60%, it is already more than 95% for an order size of euro 10 million. Besides, it can be clearly recognized that deliverable federal securities are traded more frequently OTC than nondeliverable federal securities. Exchange trades with a volume lower than euro 10 million are rarely observed. This natural threshold value might be due to the trading activities of the German Bundesbank, which is the most important counterparty for institutional investors and banks at the exchanges with their daily market holdings kept for market management purposes of up to a maximum of euro 10 million for each exchange and issue.[49] Without the trading activity of the German Bundesbank, the number of trades in German federal securities at the exchanges would clearly decrease and the average trade size would drop substantially.

Figure 2.4: Probability of an OTC Transaction Dependant on Nominal Trade Volume for Deliverable and Nondeliverable Federal Securities

This figure shows the fitted probability for an OTC trade in deliverable and nondeliverable bonds with different nominal trade volumes. The fitted probability is based on the regression results in Table 2.2. All other explanatory variables besides deliverability and nominal trading volume are held constant at their arithmetic mean.

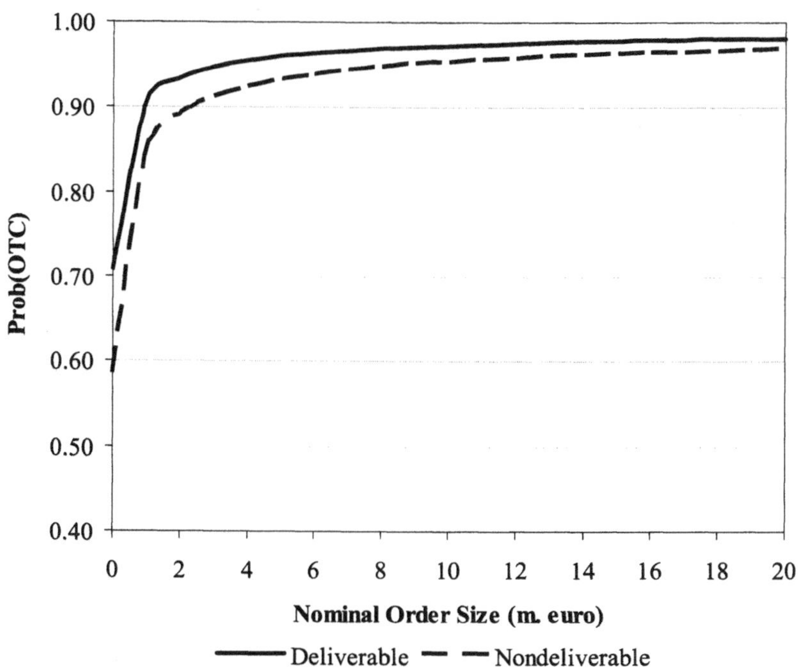

[49] On behalf of the issuer, the Federal Republic of Germany, the German Bundesbank daily engages in so-called market management activities. They have the purpose to satisfy short term liquidity requirements of the Federal Ministry of Finance. The daily market holdings per issue kept for these market management operations were between euro 3 million and euro 10 million for each exchange. See German Bundesbank (2000), p. 46 and pp. 56-57, and Kesy (2003), pp. 38-39.

Figure 2.5: Probability of an OTC Transaction Dependant on Issued Amount and Time to Maturity for Deliverable and Nondeliverable Federal Securities

This figure shows the fitted probability for an OTC trade in deliverable and nondeliverable bonds with different issued amounts. The fitted probability is based on the regression results in Table 2.2. All other explanatory variables besides deliverability and issued amount are held constant at their arithmetic mean.

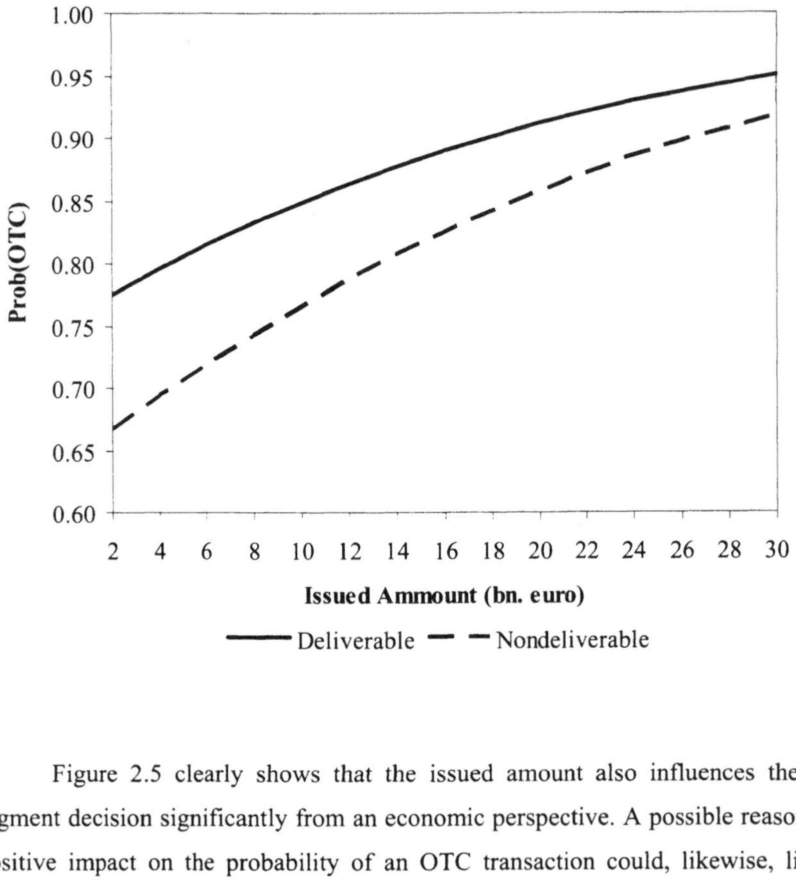

Figure 2.5 clearly shows that the issued amount also influences the trading segment decision significantly from an economic perspective. A possible reason for the positive impact on the probability of an OTC transaction could, likewise, lie in the trading activity of the German Bundesbank. Since the nominal volume potentially available for trade is smaller with small issues than with large issues, the German Bundesbank offers a relative high portion of these issues to other market participants at the exchanges within the context of its market management operations. It is conceivable that the exchange frequently offers the only possibility to acquire a significant portion of small issues. This assumption, however, cannot be conclusively confirmed with the available data. Finally, the influence of the time to maturity on the probability of an

OTC trade significant at the 90% probability level turns out to be economically negligible. This relationship is exhibited in Figure A.2.1 in the appendix to this chapter. The presumption from the robustness check is confirmed by the graphical analysis.

Altogether the estimation of our binary logit model for the customer-dealer market supports hypothesis H1. The result of the transaction-cost-theoretical considerations in Section 2.4 that absolute price risks and resultant control costs, which both increase with order size, represent the dominating criterion for trading OTC is confirmed. Additionally, the issued amount as well as the deliverability of a bond have an economically as well as a statistically significant impact on the market participants' choice of the trading segment.

2.7 Interdealer Market

2.7.1 Empirical model

Three alternative trading segment choices to execute orders exist for market participants in the interdealer market. In addition to the possibility to trade at the exchange or in the bilateral OTC market, the dealer can use the services of an independent broker in exchange for a commission fee. The following multinomial logit model tests the hypothesis H1, which was already tested for the customer dealer market, and the hypothesis H2 that, in the OTC market, the probability for a brokered interdealer trade increases with the specificity of the transaction desire:

(2.3) $$\text{Prob}(y = j \mid x) = \frac{e^{\beta_j' x}}{\sum_{j=0}^{2} e^{\beta_j' x}} \text{ for } j = 0, 1, 2$$ [50]

The dependent variable y can now take three values (j = 0, 1, 2), subjected to no logical order. It takes a value of 0 if the transaction is executed through the exchange, a value of 1 if the transaction is completed OTC bilaterally and a value of 2 if it is a brokered OTC trade. The specification of the model for interdealer market corresponds to that of the customer-dealer market from Section 2.6:

(2.4) $$x'\beta = \beta_0 + \beta_1 \cdot \log(\mathit{Size}) + \beta_2 \cdot \mathit{AmIss} + \beta_3 \cdot \mathit{Coupon} + \beta_4 \cdot \mathit{TTM} + \beta_5 \cdot \mathit{Deliv}$$

---

[50] For a detailed explanation of multinomial logit models, see, e.g., Greene (2003), pp. 719-723.

2.7.2 *Results and Interpretation*

Table 2.3 contains the results from the estimation of the model for the interdealer market. To evaluate the hypothesis H1, the estimated coefficients are represented for the reference category "exchange" ($y = 0$). The positive regression coefficients of the nominal trade size significant at the 1%-level confirm the results for the customer-dealer market. In the interdealer market, the probability that an order is executed OTC also increases in nominal order size. That applies equally to brokered OTC trades as well as to bilateral OTC transactions at a probability level of 99% in each case and confirms hypothesis H1. Therefore, the liquidity providers in the interdealer market also prefer exchange trading only for small transactions in terms of nominal value. As expected, the absolute price risks associated with exchange trades play a substantial role for the decision whether an order is executed OTC or at an exchange in the interdealer market.

The bond-specific control variables of the multinomial logit model again have a statistically significant influence on the choice of the trading segment. As in the customer-dealer market, a positive relationship between the probability for an OTC transaction and the issued amount exists. Thereby, the coefficient of the issued amount is significant for bilateral and brokered OTC trades at the 1%-level. The variables deliverability and time to maturity only influence the decision whether a transaction is executed OTC bilaterally or at an exchange. It does not, however, affect the decision between a brokered OTC trade and an exchange trade. Contrary to the customer-dealer market, a statistically significant positive influence on the choice of the trading segment also results for the coupon. Economically however, the effect of both coupon and time to maturity on the trading segment choice is negligible.[51]

[51] The analysis of the economic significance of the coupon is not reported. The economic significance of the time to maturity can be found in Figure A.2.2 in the appendix to this chapter.

Table 2.3: Estimation Results for the Interdealer Market

This table exhibits the estimation results from the multinomial logit model in Eq. (2.3). The explanatory variables are shown in Eq. (2.4). The first two columns show the results for the model estimation with exchange trade ($y = 0$) as reference category. In the third column, brokered OTC trade is the reference category. The Wald-test is applied to test the statistical significance of the regression coefficients. Respectively, ***, **, and * denote statistical significance at the 1%, 5%, and 10% level.

Reference Category	$y = 0$ (Exchange)		$y = 2$ (OTC-Brokered)
	$y = 1$ (OTC-Bilateral)	$y = 2$ (OTC-Brokered)	$y = 1$ (OTC-Bilateral)
Const	-0.869***	-3.085***	2.216***
log(Size)	0.219***	0.224***	-0.005***
AmIss	0.054***	0.021***	0.033***
Coupon	0.024**	0.008	0.016
TTM	0.015***	0.002	0.013***
Deliv	0.486***	0.013	0.473***
Pseudo-R^2 (McFadden)		0.13	
LR-χ^2 (Likelihood Ratio Test)		15,748***	
Number of Observations		91,061	

For the examination of H2, it is helpful to regard the coefficient estimates for the multinomial logit model with brokered OTC trades, $y = 1$, as reference category.[52] The regression coefficient for the nominal order size is negative and statistically significant at the 1%-level. With increasing nominal order size, the probability that the transaction will be executed bilateral OTC compared to the probability of a brokered OTC trade therefore decreases. The results derived in Section 2.4 regarding the importance of trading volume for the choice of the trading segment are thus confirmed. The independent broker represents an alternative trading segment for the dealer if the counterparty search becomes more difficult due to a high order size and, therefore, a

[52] For the reference category OTC-Brokered ($y = 2$), the coefficient estimates for the trading segment exchange ($y = 0$) are omitted since they correspond to the coefficients of the trading segment decision OTC-Brokered ($y = 2$) for the reference category exchange ($y = 0$) with reverse sign.

high liquidity demand of the transaction. Besides, an anonymous counterparty search by an independent broker can be advantageous for the dealer if the transaction contains useful information for other dealers. In the context of the empirical test of hypothesis H1 for the customer-dealer and interdealer market, the bond-specific variables only had the character of control variables. In contrast, an expected relationship in the interdealer market between the bond-related specificity variables and the probability that the decision falls to a brokered OTC trade was formulated.[53] The issued amount has the assumed effect on the trading center decision. With rising issued amount the specificity of the transaction decreases and market participants largely execute the order bilaterally instead of contracting the services of an independent broker. The coupon has no statistically significant influence on the decision OTC bilateral vs. OTC brokered. The time to maturity and deliverability of a bond, the variables with ex ante unknown sign of the impact, have both a statistically significant positive influence on the probability that the order is executed OTC bilaterally and not OTC with an independent broker as intermediary.

Based on the results of this section, hypothesis H2 can be confirmed. In the interdealer market, the coefficient estimates point out that the probability that an independent broker is assigned increases with increasing specificity of a transaction. The null hypothesis that all coefficients equal zero can be rejected at the 1%-level on the basis of the likelihood ratio test. Nevertheless, the quality of the model for the interdealer market with a McFadden-R^2 of 0.13 is relatively weak.[54] The model evaluates the determinants of the choice of the trading segment in the interdealer market based on the collected data of interdealer trades. It is however little suited for a forecast of the choice of trading segment, in particular for the differentiation between the bilateral and the brokered OTC trades. To check the robustness of the results, the model is again estimated for two subperiods. The results are shown in Tables A.2.3 and A.2.4 of the appendix. Besides the nominal order size, the issued amount and the deliverability also have a significant impact on the choice of the trading segment. The variation in the coefficient and the significance of the variable time to maturity contradicts the hypothesis of a systematic influence of this variable on the choice of trading segment.

[53] See in addition Section 2.4.

[54] See, among others, Backhaus (2003), p. 447.

In order to assess the economic significance of the determinants for the interdealer market, we also do a graphical analysis. In Figure 2.6 the probabilities for the different trading segments are plotted in dependence of the nominal trading volume. The differentiation between deliverable and nondeliverable bonds is omitted for the sake of simplicity although the influence of the deliverability is economically significant. The probability for an exchange trade decreases rapidly with increasing nominal order size, while the probability for a bilateral OTC transaction rises just as fast. Starting from the nominal volume with no more orders executed through the stock exchange, the probability of a brokered OTC transaction increases in order size and the probability for a bilateral OTC decreases with order size. While the probability for a brokered OTC trade scarcely exceeds 4% for orders with a nominal size of euro 10 million, it already amounts to over 10% of the trades with an order size of euro 200 million.

Figure 2.7 plots the probabilities for the different trading segments dependant on issued amount. Here, an economically significant influence can also be recognized. The influence of the issued amount on the decision to rely on the services of an independent broker is, however, extremely small. A graphical demonstration of the relationship between the choice of trading segment and the time to maturity can be found in Figure A.2.2 in the appendix because of the small economic relevance of this variable.

Figure 2.6: Probability of an Exchange Trade, a Bilateral OTC Trade, and a Brokered OTC Trade Dependant on Nominal Trade Volume

This figure shows the fitted probability for an exchange trade, a bilateral OTC trade, and a brokered OTC trade for different values of the nominal order size. The fitted probability is based on the regression results in Table 2.3. All other explanatory variables besides nominal order size are held constant at their arithmetic mean.

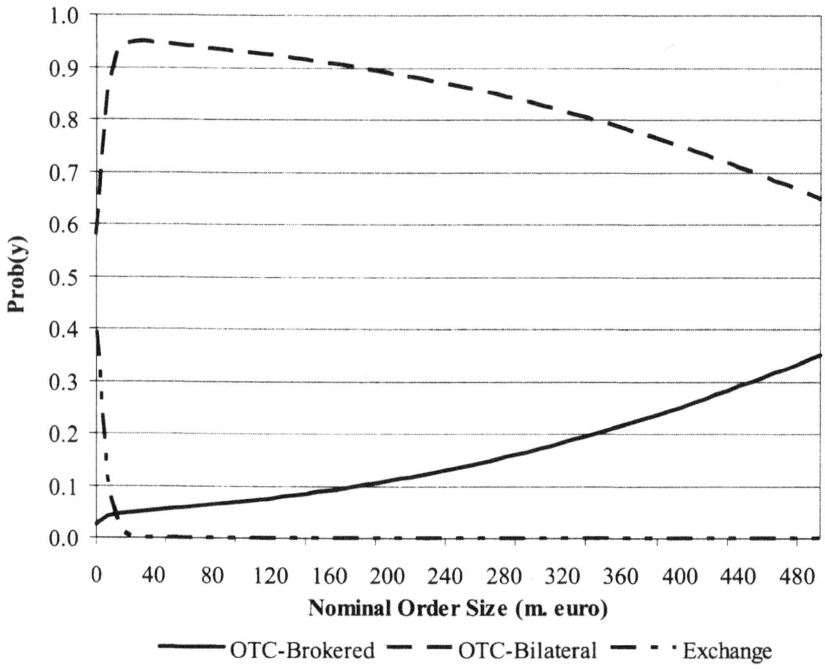

In summary, the results of the analysis of the interdealer market concerning hypothesis H1 are in line with the results from the customer-dealer market. Hypothesis H1 is thus confirmed for both market spheres. It applies that the higher the nominal order size, the higher is the probability that a market participant prefers the OTC market over the exchange due to the resulting price risks.

Figure 2.7: Probability of an Exchange Trade, a Bilateral OTC Trade, and a Brokered OTC Trade Dependant on Issued Amount

This figure shows the fitted probability for an exchange trade, a bilateral OTC trade, and a brokered OTC trade for different values of the nominal trade volume. The fitted probability is based on the regression results in Table 2.3. All other explanatory variables besides issued amount are held constant at their arithmetic mean.

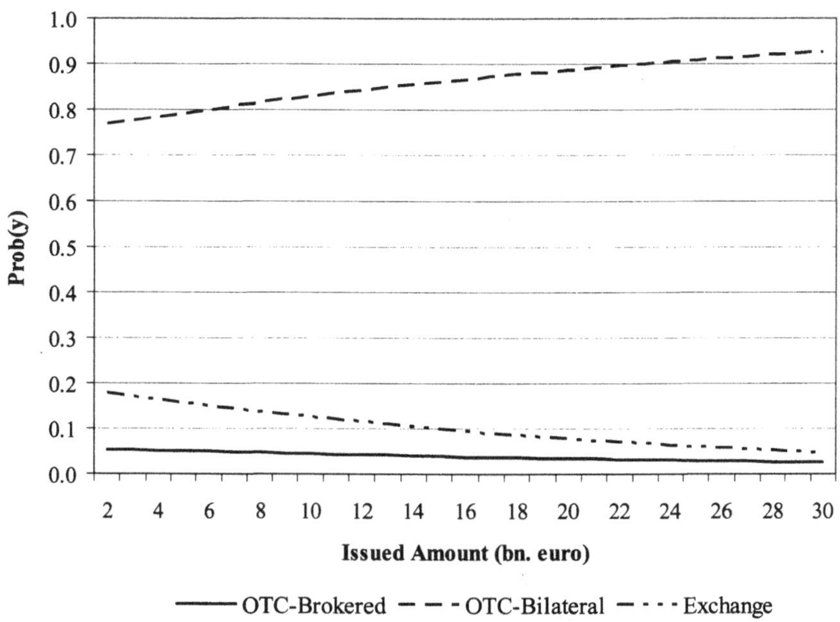

Hypothesis H2 is generally confirmed by the results of the model estimation for the interdealer market. Nominal trade volume, issued amount and deliverability of the traded bond into a Eurex futures contract are identified as the most important determinants of the choice of OTC trading segments. Our analysis of the interdealer market points to the conclusion that in the OTC trading segment, the probability of a brokered trade increases with increasing transaction specificity. Therefore, it can be concluded that at least some of the market participants in the interdealer market accredit an added value to the services – counterparty search and anonymity – of an independent broker for trades with certain characteristics.

2.8 Conclusion

This article analyzes for the first time the phenomenon of the coexistence of several trading segments in the field of bond trading. In the secondary market for German federal securities, we observe over decades grown on- and off-exchange market structures and raise the question whether these can be justified economically or whether manifested institutional conditions conserve the historically grown market structure. The three existing parallel trading segments – exchange trading, bilateral OTC trading, and brokered OTC trading - exhibit substantial differences regarding the price formation mechanism and anonymity of the counterparties. Therefore our initial hypothesis is that each trading mechanism fulfills its own function for the market participants and attracts different transaction desires. We obtain significant empirical results, indicating that the three different trading possibilities are not seen as interchangeable trading segments by the market participants. Instead, each secondary market segment satisfies different transaction needs. In summary, our analysis shows that the prevailing structure of the secondary market for German federal securities with several differently organized trading segments is justified on the basis of economic considerations. Institutional conditions do not seem to be the main cause for the existence of the different trading segments.

For the secondary market for German federal securities it can be assumed that, in the future, the proportion of bilateral OTC transactions will still continue to increase particularly debited to the brokered OTC transactions. This is because of the progressive development and dissemination of electronic trading systems. The forecasted loss of importance of independent brokers working on a commission basis relies on the observation that meanwhile in the interdealer market, electronic trading systems exist which make an anonymous bilateral trading possible.[55] Since they have also lost a crucial competitive advantage with the loss of the unique position as anonymity provider, we assume a reduction of the brokered OTC trades already occurred and this development will continue.

Due to its organization as auction market, the potential of the exchange trading is limited to transactions with small absolute trading volumes. Larger trade volumes at

[55] Anonymous electronic interdealer trading systems are usually those systems that operate via cross matching methods like eSpeed, Inc., Eurex Bonds, or ICAP. See The Bond Market Association (2005a), p. 5.

the exchange might primarily be the result of the market activities of the German Bundesbank traditionally implemented over the German exchanges. Without daily market management operations and the resulting daily exchange trading of the German Bundesbank as a contractor for institutional market participants, exchange members would presumably use the exchange floor only as a trading platform for retail customer orders and very small institutional trades.

Appendix to Part 2

Table A.2.1: Estimation Results for the Customer-Dealer Market (January 2, 2001 – April 2, 2001)

This table exhibits the results from the model in Eq. (2.1) estimated for the period from January 2, 2001 until April 2, 2001. The explanatory variables are shown in Eq. (2.2). The variable coupon was omitted from the model estimation since it proved insignificant. The Wald-test is applied to test the statistical significance of the regression coefficients. Respectively, ***, **, and * denote statistical significance at the 1%, 5%, and 10% level.

	$y = 1$ (OTC)
Const	0.904***
log(Size)	0.602***
AmIss	0.058***
TTM	0.009***
Deliv	0.640***
Pseudo-R^2 (McFadden)	0.43
LR-χ^2 (Likelihood Ratio Test)	27,490***
Number of Observations	53,352

Table A.2.2: Estimation Results for the Customer-Dealer Market (April 3, 2001 – June 29, 2001)

This table exhibits the results from the logit model in Eq. (2.1) estimated for the period from April 3, 2001 until June 29, 2001. The explanatory variables are shown in Eq. (2.2). The variable coupon was omitted from the model estimation since it proved insignificant. The Wald-test is applied to test the statistical significance of the regression coefficients. Respectively, ***, **, and * denote statistical significance at the 1%, 5%, and 10% level.

	$y = 1$ (OTC)
Const	0.920***
log(Size)	0.557***S
AmIss	0.067***
TTM	0.007***
Deliv	0.441***
Pseudo-R^2 (McFadden)	0.39
LR-χ^2 (Likelihood Ratio Test)	21,065***
Number of Observations	44,716

Table A.2.3: Estimation Results for the Interdealer Market (January 2, 2001 – April 2, 2001)

This table exhibits the results from the multinomial logit model in Eq. (2.3) estimated for the period from January 2, 2001 until April 2, 2001. The explanatory variables are shown in Eq. (2.4). The first two columns show the results for the model estimation with exchange trade (y = 0) as reference category. In the third column, brokered OTC trade is the reference category. The Wald-test is applied to test the statistical significance of the regression coefficients. Respectively, ***, **, and * denote statistical significance at the 1%, 5%, and 10% level.

Reference Category	$y = 0$ (Exchange)		$y = 2$ (OTC-Brokered)
	y = 1 (OTC-Bilateral)	y = 2 (OTC-Brokered)	$y = 1$ (OTC-Bilateral)
Const	-0.925***	-3.315***	2.390***
log(Size)	0.222***	0.227***	-0.004***
AmIss	0.057***	0.036***	0.020***
Coupon	0.016	0.021	-0.005
TTM	0.020***	-0.008**	0.028***
Deliv	0.521***	-0.039	0.561***
Pseudo-R^2 (McFadden)		0.14	
LR-χ^2 (Likelihood Ratio Test)		9,543***	
Number of Observations		52,587	

Table A.2.4: Estimation Results for the Interdealer Market (April 3, 2001 – June 29, 2001)

This table exhibits the results from the multinomial logit model in Eq. (2.3) estimated for the period from April 3, 2001 until June 29, 2001. The explanatory variables are shown in Eq. (2.4). The first two columns show the results for the model estimation with exchange trade (y = 0) as reference category. In the third column, brokered OTC trade is the reference category. The Wald-test is applied to test the statistical significance of the regression coefficients. Respectively, ***, **, and * denote statistical significance at the 1%, 5%, and 10% level.

Reference Category	$y = 0$ (Exchange)		$y = 2$ (OTC-Brokered)
	y = 1 (OTC-Bilateral)	y = 2 (OTC-Brokered)	$y = 1$ (OTC-Bilateral)
Const	-0.003	-2.003***	2.000***
log(Size)	0.315***	0.375***	-0.060***
AmIss	0.044***	-0.004	0.006***
Coupon	0.031**	-0.013	0.044
TTM	0.007***	0.011***	-0.004
Deliv	0.442***	-0.063	0.378***
Pseudo-R^2 (McFadden)		0.08	
LR-χ^2 (Likelihood Ratio Test)		4,365***	
Number of Observations		38,474	

Figure A.2.1: Probability of an OTC Transaction Dependant on Time to Maturity for Deliverable and Nondeliverable Federal Securities

This figure shows the fitted probability for an OTC trade in deliverable and nondeliverable bonds with different values of time to maturity. The fitted probability is based on the regression results in Table 2.2. All other explanatory variables besides deliverability and time to maturity are held constant at their arithmetic mean.

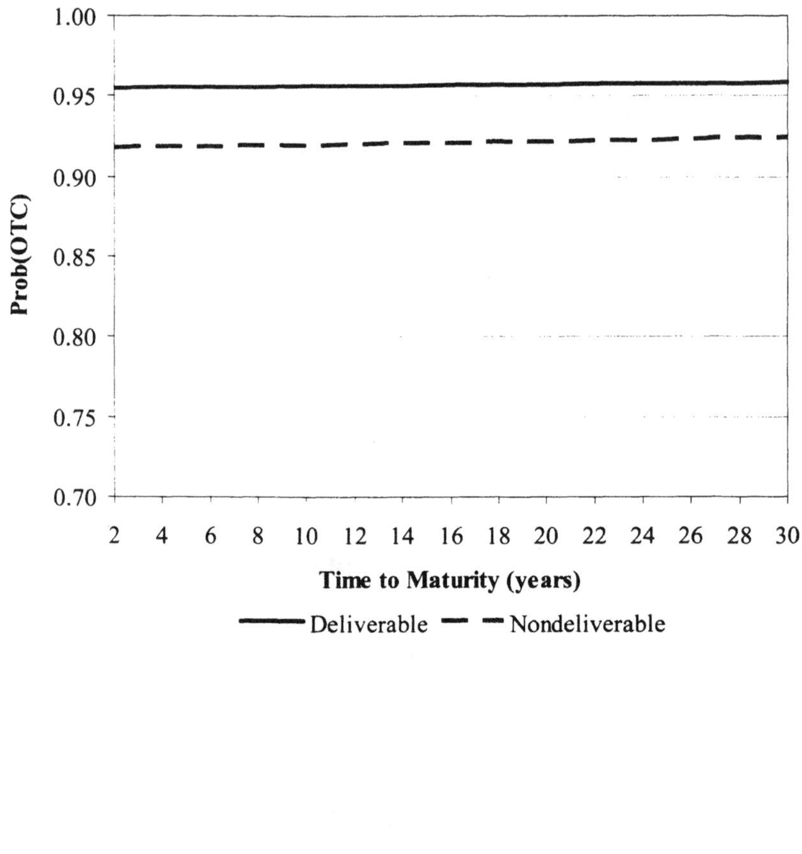

Figure A.2.2: Probability of an Exchange Trade, a Bilateral OTC Trade, and a Brokered OTC Trade Dependant on Time to Maturity

This figure shows the fitted probability for an exchange trade, a bilateral OTC trade, and a brokered OTC trade for different values of the time to maturity. The fitted probability is based on the regression results in Table 2.3. All other explanatory variables besides time to maturity are held constant at their arithmetic mean.

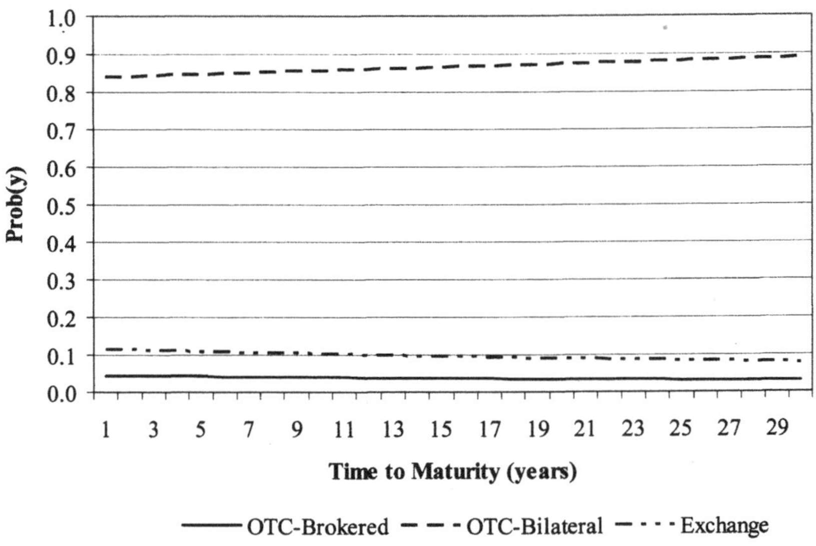

3 Interdealer versus Customer-Dealer Sphere: Information Processing in Decentralized Multiple-Dealership Markets

3.1 Introduction

This paper empirically analyzes the short-run price dynamics in the European government bond market. One distinguishing feature of bond markets is the coexistence of two different trading environments: a public environment where customers (buy side investors) trade with liquidity providers, and an interdealer environment where liquidity providers trade among themselves.[56] The objective of the statistical analysis is to quantify the contribution of each market to the evolution of a bond's full-information or permanent value. From an economic perspective, these contributions specify how much information is produced in the various markets, which may be related to security and market characteristics. Our analysis particularly addresses the following questions: Which market contributes more to the price discovery - the customer-dealer or the interdealer market? Is the share of the contribution to the price discovery of both markets related to security characteristics? The market for government bonds is especially suited to answer the last question since it includes a wide variety of similar but not identical issues (the issues differ in amount outstanding, maturity, and other characteristics). The question about price discovery, market sphere, and security characteristics could not be fully examined if we were inspecting different markets for a single security.

To our knowledge, this paper is the first addressing the relationship between interdealer and customer-dealer markets in multiple-dealership environments. Related literature focuses on the comparison of the efficiency of electronic trading and open outcry systems. The first set of studies in this field comprises Shyy and Lee (1995), Kofman and Moser (1997), Martens (1998), and Tse and Zabotina (2001). They either compare the Bund future prices of the open outcry system at the London International Futures Exchange (LIFFE) with the prices of the electronic trading mechanism at Deutsche Terminbörse (DTB) or, like Tse and Zabotina (2001), analyze the FTSE 100 before and after the transition from open outcry to electronic screen trading. Shyy and Lee (1995) find mixed results, with LIFFE being the more dominant market.[57] On the

---

56 See Gravelle (2002), p. 7.

57 See Shyy and Lee (1995), p. 94.

other hand, Kofman and Moser (1997) find that DTB is leading.[58] Martens (1998), who uses the same price contribution measure as we do, divides his sample in subperiods with high and low volatility. In high volatility periods, LIFFE, the open-outcry system, has the largest share in the price discovery process, while in low volatility periods the DTB contributes most to the price discovery process. This pattern reflects the fact, that at LIFFE, the only information comes from trading, whereas the limit order book provides important information also in the absence of trading.[59] Applying Hasbrouck's (1993) model, Tse and Zabotina (2001) find a higher quality and pricing efficiency in the open outcry system. Additionally, the information content of trades in the open outcry market is higher.[60] A second set of articles examines the price discovery process in equity index futures traded under different trading mechanisms. Hasbrouck (2003) analyzes the price discovery process between regular index futures (floor trading), E-mini index futures (electronic trading), and Exchange Traded Funds in the S&P 500 and the NASDAQ 100 indexes. He finds that most of the price discovery occurs in the E-mini futures market.[61] Using the same indexes as in Hasbrouck (2003), Kurov and Lasser (2004) also find that price discovery is initiated in the E-mini futures market. Interestingly, it is driven by trades of floor traders who can also access the E-mini index futures market.[62] Ates and Wang (2005) show for the S&P 500 and NASDAQ 100 index futures markets, that one year after the introduction of the E-mini future, its price contribution has been greater than that of the regular index future for both markets. They cannot support the hypothesis that electronic trading contributes a larger proportion in information shares during low volatility periods.[63]

Although some aspects are similar to the questions investigated by the above reviewed literature, this article differs in some important points. In existing literature, all investors have the possibility to trade in all of the analyzed markets. In bond markets, however, buy-side investors do not have access to the interdealer environment and act solely as liquidity-demanders. They cannot disseminate quotes through electronic information systems. In both markets, dealers are the only market participants providing quotes and individual customer-trades are negotiated with one of the dealers. The trade

[58] See Kofman and Moser (1997), p. 291.
[59] See Martens (1998), pp. 252-256.
[60] See Tse and Zabotina (2001), pp. 725-731.
[61] See Hasbrouck (2003), pp. 2387-2390.
[62] See Kurov and Lasser (2004), pp. 374-381.
[63] See Ates and Wang (2005), p. 681.

motivation is also different in the two markets. While investors in the customer-dealer market mainly trade on expectations regarding future changes in the yield curve, dealers in the interdealer-market trade with other dealers to rebalance their inventories in response to customer trading.[64] Therefore, answering the first question (Which market contributes more to the price discovery?) also gives an answer to the question which market is used by the dealers to convey their information first. This may in turn be related to the organizational structure of both markets.

The results are particularly interesting for market participants in decentralized multiple dealership markets like FX (foreign exchange) or bond markets. Both markets share the common feature of two trading environments. Investors as well as liquidity providers can use both markets as a source for price information. Especially in times when new information arrives at the market, market participants try to avoid pricing errors. Therefore, they are interested in each market's contribution to the price formation, temporary and permanent price effects in both markets, how the markets are interrelated, whether the results are different for different securities, and whether these differences can be explained by security characteristics. The results are also important for regulators, people involved in designing markets, or other parties concerned with market stability. Poor price discovery may result in higher price volatility, including bubbles or sudden market crashes when prices are predominantly influenced by short-run disturbances, and market designers are interested in the question whether different market structures are optimal for securities with different characteristics.

Price discovery is defined as the process of impounding new information into an asset's full-information or permanent price. The permanent price is unobservable but the observable price can be decomposed into its fundamental value and its transient effects. While changes in the fundamental value are due to new information, transient effects are probably microstructure related effects.[65] To decompose these effects and to measure the contribution to the price discovery of each of the two markets, we adopt Hasbrouck's (1995, 2003) methodology.[66]

---

64 See Gravelle (2002), p. 7 for bond markets and Lyons (1995), p. 323 for FX markets.

65 See, e.g., Hasbrouck (1995), p. 1175 and p. 1182, and Hasbrouck (2002), pp. 329-330.

66 For an overview on Hasbrouck's information share measure see Hasbrouck (1995), pp. 1178-1184, and Hasbrouck (2003), pp. 2382-2384.

Hasbrouck's (1995, 2003) information share measure is applied to a unique integrated dataset of time stamped high-frequency quotes from both, the customer-dealer and the interdealer market. For the customer-dealer market, indicative quotes for a sample of 24 different dealers were collected from Bloomberg L.P., while for the interdealer market tradable EuroMTS quotes were recorded from the same information system. Overall, our dataset consists of quotes for 58 trading days between September 30, 2003 and December 19, 2003 in 114 government bonds issued by members of the EMU (European Monetary Union).

We find that the customer-dealer market dominates the price discovery of our sample of very liquid government bonds. Nevertheless, EuroMTS also has a significant share in the price discovery process. Using cross section regressions, we find that the contribution to the price discovery of EuroMTS varies with the liquidity of the bond. The information share of the electronic trading system EuroMTS is larger for illiquid bonds than for liquid bonds. Although EuroMTS dominates the price discovery only for a few bonds in the sample, the findings suggest that the share of EuroMTS in the price discovery process may be larger than the customer-dealer market's share for less liquid bonds not covered by our data.

The remainder of the paper is organized as follows. Section 3.2 provides an overview on the customer-dealer and the interdealer market for European government bonds and derives the hypotheses. The methodology used in this article is reviewed in Section 3.3. Section 3.4 discusses practical problems that arise. An overview on the data and descriptive statistics is provided in section 3.5. Section 3.6 discusses the estimation results and impulse response functions and section 3.7 relates the information share estimates to the liquidity of the bonds. Finally, Section 3.8 concludes.

3.2 Markets and Hypotheses

3.2.1 The Customer-Dealer and the Interdealer Market for European Government Bonds

One obvious difference between the interdealer market, especially EuroMTS, and the customer-dealer market is their organizational structure. The customer-dealer sphere is still very opaque. Each dealer posts bid- and ask-quotes through electronic information systems like Bloomberg. Unlike in multiple-dealership equity markets (e.g. NASDAQ), this information is not available on a fully consolidated basis on one screen. Additionally, the quotes in the customer-dealer government bond market are only indicative.[67] Volume is rarely posted and post-trade information is usually not available either.[68] To obtain a tradable quote, a customer needs to contact a dealer directly by phone, email, or via electronic trading platforms to make a so-called firm quote request.

Interdealer trading is much more centralized. The vast majority of trading takes place on a small number of multi-dealer platforms.[69] Not only the concentration but also the transparency is higher in interdealer markets. The EuroMTS system, for example, effectively works like a limit order book with tradable quotes. One interesting feature is that the liquidity providers, who post quotes, are the same in both markets. Every dealer offering liquidity in the customer-dealer market also trades in the interdealer market to share the unwanted inventory due to customer trades.[70]

3.2.2 Hypotheses

From a macroeconomic perspective, only public information is relevant in government bond markets. Macroeconomic indicators, which are used by economists and market participants to determine bond prices, are publicly announced to all market participants at the same time, and can be impounded into prices directly. From a microstructure perspective, private information exists in government bond markets as well. This information is the customer order flow observed by each dealer. It is private because only the parties involved (dealer and customer) have knowledge on the existence of the trade and its conditions (price and volume). In fact, several analyses of the FX market illustrate that order flow conveys information.[71] In addition, FX dealers agree that small

---

67 Recent literature on indicative quotes provides evidence that indicative quotes do contain information and, therefore, do not have the sole purpose to attract customers. See, e.g., Biais, Hillion and Spatt (1999), and Cao, Ghysels and Hatheway (2000).

68 An exception is post-trade information on trades conducted via single-dealer platforms. The information is not available to the broad public, but is usually distributed to the platforms' subscribers.

69 The Bond Market Association identifies four important interdealer systems for European bonds. See The Bond Market Association (2005a), p. 9.

70 See Gravelle (2002), p. 7 for bond markets and Lyons (1995), p. 323 for FX markets.

71 For the evidence that foreign exchange order flow conveys information, see, e.g., Lyons (1995), Ito, Lyons, and Melvin (1998), Cheung and Wong (2000), Naranjo and Nimalendran (2000), and Evans (2002).

liquidity providers with only little customer order flow have a hard time in the market.[72] To offset their unwanted inventory subsequent to a customer trade, dealers use the interdealer environment instead of waiting for offsetting customer trades. This risk sharing behavior in interdealer markets leads to the well known phenomenon of hot potato trading.[73] Although hot potato trading may decelerate the impounding of order flow information into prices, dealers learn about other dealers' order flow only through interdealer trading. In fact, prices have to depend on trades in the interdealer market since dealers cannot observe other dealers customer trades.[74] Lyons (2001) concludes that information is first revealed in the interdealer market and that the interdealer market leads the customer-dealer market slightly.[75] Therefore, we expect the interdealer market to have a larger share in the price discovery process than the customer dealer market, which is our first hypothesis.

H1: The share in the price discovery process of the interdealer market is larger than the share of the customer dealer market.

As outlined in Section 1, electronic trading is especially efficient in times of low information intensity and open outcry mechanisms have a larger share in the price discovery process in times of high volatility.[76] In analogy, we would expect that the interdealer market contributes more to the price discovery process for illiquid bonds than for liquid bonds.

H2: The information share is related to securities' characteristics. The information share of the interdealer market is higher for illiquid bonds.

---

72 See Goodhart (1988), pp. 456-457, Lyons (1997), p. 279, and Lyons (2001), p. 45.

73 For a review on hot-potato trading see Lyons (1996a,b), and Lyons (1997). Hot potato trading arises because the risk-averse dealers have no ex ante knowledge of which dealers are long and which dealers are short. Additionally, they cannot condition on other dealers' trades. Perfect efficient risk sharing between dealers is therefore not possible. See Lyons (2001), p. 102.

74 See Lyons (1997), p. 279 and Lyons (2001), p. 96.

75 See Lyons (2001), p. 115.

76 A review on the literature on the efficiency of electronic trading and open outcry systems can be found in Section 3.1.

Intuitively, more illiquid bonds are less frequently traded. As a result, it is more difficult to get information from customer trades because they are relatively inactive in these bonds. Their behavior does not reveal much about their intentions and, thus, does not permit reliable predictions of their activities over the next period. Quotes on EuroMTS on the other hand are tradeable and offer more signals for predicting market developments.[77]

With 114 similar but not identical securities, our data is the first that allows us to isolate security related effects on the information share of quotes in different market structures.

3.3 Methodology

When a security is traded in more than one market, common factor models can be used to measure the markets' contributions to the price discovery process. The alternative models of Gonzalo and Granger (1995) and Hasbrouck (1995) provide different views of the price discovery process between markets.[78] Hasbrouck's model considers each market's contribution to the variance of the implicit efficient price (common to all markets). Relying on the premise that the flow of information is reflected by volatility, he defines the share of a market in the price discovery process as the proportion of the variation in the efficient price innovation attributable to that market.[79] Gonzalo and Granger (1995) decompose the common factor itself. The leading role in the price discovery process is attributed to the market that adjusts least to the price movement in the other market.[80] While Hasbrouck's model accounts for correlation between markets, Gonzalo and Granger (1995) neglect any correlation between the markets. Baillie et al. (2002) show that both models are directly related. Therefore, both measures should produce similar results.[81] Baillie et al. (2002) also conclude that a final judgment that one of the two models provides a better measure of price discovery cannot be made since it depends on whether price discovery is considered to be solely an error

77 See, e.g., Martens (1998), pp. 246-247.

78 An overview on both models is presented in a collection of papers: Baillie et al. (2002), de Jong (2002), Harris, McInish, and Wood (2002), Hasbrouck (2002), Hasbrouck (2003), and Lehmann (2002).

79 See Hasbrouck (1995), p. 1177.

80 See Gonzalo and Granger (1995), p. 7 and Baillie et al. (2002), p. 320.

81 Other authors apply both measures to their data and find similar results. See e.g. Ates and Wang (2005), p. 709.

correction phenomenon or whether it should also consider the correlations among markets.[82] Taking correlations into account and assuming that information is reflected by volatility is the more general approach. Therefore, the Hasbrouck (1995) information share approach is applied for the prevailing analysis.

3.3.1 Cointegration

The analysis follows Hasbrouck's (1995) information share approach and is based on the econometrics of cointegrated vector autoregressions.[83] It focuses on the random-walk components in a set of security prices, i.e. the remainders after transient effects have been removed. In our case where one underlying security is traded in different markets, the random-walk component is the same for the prices in all markets. The variance of the random-walk innovation is decomposed into components attributable to innovations in each markets price series. The relative contribution of a given price to this variance is defined as that price's information share.

Let $p_t = [p_{1t} \quad p_{2t} \quad \ldots \quad p_{nt}]'$ be a $(n \times 1)$ vector of nonstationary prices. Nonstationarity implies that the future time path of the prices depends on past effects. More specifically, assume that all prices follow a random walk so that they are integrated of order one $I(1)$. This means that the first differences $\Delta p_{1t}, \Delta p_{2t}, \ldots, \Delta p_{nt}$ are $I(0)$ and are stationary processes.

Although the prices are individually nonstationary, we expect them to be related to one another if they are all prices for the same underlying asset. In other words, we expect that the prices are linked by one or more linear arbitrage relationships. In the bivariate case, for example, where p_{1t} is the bid-price and p_{2t} is the ask-price, the difference $p_{1t} - p_{2t}$ does not diverge over time. Formally, the prices are said to be cointegrated.[84] Define $\mu = E(p_{1t} - p_{2t})$ as the mean deviation. In the case of bid- and ask-prices, μ is the average quoted spread and represents the round trip costs of buying and selling one share. In the parlance of time series econometrics, $(p_{1t} - p_{2t}) - \mu$ is called the "error". In the example with bid- and ask-prices, the error might be interpreted as the deviation from the average round trip costs, because of large trading volume or

---

82 Baillie et al. (2002), p. 313.

83 A textbook discussion of cointegration is provided by Hamilton (1994), pp. 571-629.

84 For the exact definition of cointegration, see Engle and Granger (1987), p. 253.

intraday patterns. More generally, if there are n price series, there are n–1 linearly independent differences. It is convenient to define these as

$$(3.1) \qquad z_t = [(p_{1t} - p_{2t})(p_{1t} - p_{3t})\cdots(p_{1t} - p_{nt})]'.$$

The reduced form econometric specification underlying the analysis is a vector error correction model (VECM) of order M:[85]

$$(3.2) \qquad \Delta p_t = B_1 \Delta p_{t-1} + B_2 \Delta p_{t-2} + \cdots + B_M \Delta p_{t-M} + \gamma(z_{t-1} - \mu) + \varepsilon_t .$$

Δp_t is the column vector of prices, the B_i matrices are autoregressive coefficients for lag $i = 1$ to M, $\gamma(z_{t-1} - \mu)$ is the error correction term, γ is an adjustment coefficient, and ε_t is a zero-mean vector of serially uncorrelated innovations with covariance matrix

$$(3.3) \qquad \Omega = \begin{pmatrix} \sigma_1^2 & \sigma_{12} \\ \sigma_{21} & \sigma_2^2 \end{pmatrix}.$$

The VECM has two portions: the first portion, $\Sigma B_i \Delta p_{t-i}$, depicts the short-run dynamics between the price series induced by market imperfections, while the second portion, $\gamma(z_{t-1} - \mu)$, represents the long-run or equilibrium dynamics between the price series. In our case Δp_t is the 2×1 vector of interdealer and customer prices, B_i are 2×2 matrices

$$(3.4) \qquad B = \begin{bmatrix} a_{11} & a_{12} \\ a_{21} & a_{22} \end{bmatrix},$$

z_{t-1} is the difference between the two prices, $p_{1t} - p_{2t}$, with $\mu = E(z_{t-1})$, and γ is the 2×1 vector of speed of adjustment coefficients

$$(3.5) \qquad \gamma = \begin{bmatrix} \gamma_{1,2} \\ \gamma_{2,1} \end{bmatrix}.$$

Alternatively, the stationary price difference can be represented as $z_{t-1} = \beta' p_t$ with $\beta = [1 \ \text{-}1]$.

---

[85] This equation follows the Granger Representation Theorem. See Engle and Granger (1987), pp. 255-256.

Even though the VECM is relatively easy to estimate, the parameters are difficult to interpret in the reduced form specification. It is more useful to examine the impulse response functions which characterize the joint price dynamics subsequent to initial shocks to the individual component prices, and the information shares.

3.3.2 *Impulse Response Function*

Engle and Granger (1987) show that the VECM representation in Eq. (3.2) shares an equivalent moving average representation:

$$(3.6) \qquad \Delta p_t = \Psi(L)\varepsilon_t = \varepsilon_t + \psi_1\varepsilon_{t-1} + \psi_2\varepsilon_{t-2} + \psi_3\varepsilon_{t-3} + \ldots,$$

where ε_t is the vector of zero-mean innovations with Var(ε_t) = Ω and E($\varepsilon_t\,\varepsilon'_s$) = 0 for $t \neq s$, and Ψ is a polynomial in the lag operator, $L(\cdot)_t = (\cdot)_{t-1}$. The ψ_i are $n \times n$ coefficient matrices.[86]

The common trend representation of the cointegrated system follows directly from Eq. (3.6). Adding and subtracting $\Psi(1)\varepsilon_t$ from the right hand side of (3.6) yields

$$(3.7) \qquad \Delta p_t = \Psi(1)\varepsilon_t + [\Psi(L) - \Psi(1)]\varepsilon_t.$$

Solving backwards for the level of p_t gives

$$(3.8) \qquad p_t = \Psi(1)\sum_{s=1}^{t}\varepsilon_s + \Psi^*(L)\varepsilon_t + p_0,$$

where p_0 is a constant, $\Psi(L)$ and $\Psi^*(L)$ are matrix polynomials in the lag operator, L. The impact matrix, $\Psi(1)$, is the sum of the moving average coefficients, with $\Psi(1)\varepsilon_t$ being the long-run impact of an innovation on each of the prices. p_0 is a vector of initial values that may reflect nonstochastic differences between the price variables, and the second term in Eq. (3.8) is a zero mean covariance stationary process – the "transitory" component. Eq. (3.8) is also called the multivariate Beveridge-Nelson (1981) decomposition of p_t.[87] The stationarity of $\beta' p_t$ implies that $\beta'\Psi(1) = 0$.[88] Since β = [1 -1],

[86] See Engle and Granger (1987), pp. 255-256.

[87] See Stock and Watson (1988), p. 1098 and Watson (1994), pp. 2872-2874. The univariate Beveridge-Nelson decompostition can be found in Beveridge and Nelson (1981), pp. 154-158.

this implies that the rows of the impact matrix are identical. Therefore, the long-run impact is the same for all prices. If we denote $\psi = (\psi_1, \psi_2)$ as the common row vector in $\Psi(1)$, Eq. (3.8) becomes

$$p_t = \psi\left(\sum_{s=1}^{t} \varepsilon_s\right)\iota + \Psi^*(L)\varepsilon_t + p_0, \tag{3.9}$$

where $\iota = (1\ 1)'$ is a column vector of ones.

The increment $\psi\varepsilon_t$ in Eq. (3.9) is the permanent component of the price change common to all prices and presumably due to new information. Not included are transient effects that may be attributed e.g. to bid-ask bounces or inventory adjustments. Hasbrouck (1995) defines this component to be the common efficient price (common factor) between the two prices.[89]

The impact matrix $\Psi(1)$ is calculated directly from the VECM in Eq. (3.2) by stepping the system forward in response to a one-unit innovation.[90] The basic idea is to set the model at rest for a period equal to the longest lag in the specification (in our case 5 minutes). Then, one of the prices is perturbed and the response of both prices for a specified number of time steps in the future is forecasted. Consider the system in Eq. (3.2) with $\Delta p_t = 0$ and $z_t = \mu$ for $t = -1, -2, \ldots$. At time $t = 0$, suppose there is a shock of $\varepsilon_0 = [1\ 0]'$ in our bivariate system. Then,

$$\begin{aligned} \Delta p_0 &= \begin{bmatrix} 1 \\ 0 \end{bmatrix} \\ z_0 &= \mu + \beta'\Delta p_0 \\ \Delta p_1 &= B_1\Delta p_0 + \gamma z_0 \\ z_1 &= z_0 + \beta'\Delta p_1 \\ \Delta p_2 &= B_1\Delta p_0 + B_2\Delta p_0 + \gamma z_0 \\ &\vdots \end{aligned} \tag{3.10}$$

88 A violation of this implication also violates the assumption of a stationary cointegration vector. Let one stock be traded at two different exchanges. In the absence of arbitrage opportunities, the prices at both exchanges are cointegrated and the difference in the prices is a covariance stationary process. If $\beta'\Psi(1) \neq 0$, a shock to the price at one exchange leads to a disequilibrium in the long-run and, therefore, a permanent arbitrage opportunity.

89 See Hasbrouck (1995), pp. 1180-1181.

90 See Hamilton (1994), pp. 318-323.

The first column of B_0 is Δp_0, the first column of B_1 is Δp_1, and so forth. To obtain the second column of B_0, B_1, etc., we repeat the procedure and forecast the system subsequently to an initial shock of $\varepsilon_0 = [0\ 1]'$. The impulse response functions are obtained by graphing the Δp_i (or the columns of ψ_i) against i and the cumulative impulse response function $\Psi(1)$ is obtained from the sum of the individual ψ_i matrices. The plots of the impulse response functions are very useful in summarizing and interpreting the price dynamics.

3.3.3 Information Share Measure

Following Hasbrouck (1995, 2003), the increment $\psi\varepsilon_t$ is the component of the price change that is permanently impounded into the security price. Since $\mathrm{Var}(\varepsilon_t) = \Omega$, the variance of the common factor innovations can be expressed as

$$(3.11) \qquad \mathrm{var}(\psi\varepsilon_t) = \psi\Omega\psi'.$$

If the market innovations are uncorrelated and Ω is thus diagonal, $\psi\Omega\psi'$ will consist of n terms, each of which represents the contribution to the random-walk innovation from one market. The information share IS_j is then defined as the proportion of this for market j relative to the total variance of the random-walk innovation from a particular market

$$(3.12) \qquad IS_j = \psi_j^2\Omega_{jj} / \psi\Omega\psi'.$$

If the innovation covariance matrix is not diagonal ($\sigma_{12} \neq 0$), the information share is not exactly identified and Eq. (3.12) does not hold. In this case, a Cholesky factorization of Ω provides upper and lower bounds. The Cholesky factorization of Ω results in a lower triangular matrix M that satisfies $\Omega = \mathrm{MM}'$. The matrix M can be used to construct orthogonalized innovations, $u_{j,t} = \mathrm{M}^{-1}\varepsilon_{j,t}$, and provides the new information share measure for market j

$$(3.13) \qquad IS_j = ([\psi M]_j)^2 / \psi\Omega\psi'.$$

The information share measure places the majority of the variance on the innovations in the first column of the innovation matrix. In the bivariate case, the upper (lower) bound of the information share is obtained by putting the market j the first (second) variable in the factorization.[91] The bounds tighten as the diagonal case is approached, i.e. as the magnitude of the off-diagonal covariance σ_{12} decreases. Intuitively, if the price innovations are highly correlated, it is not possible to assign explanatory power with any precision. In practical terms, this suggests employing a very fine time resolution to avoid introducing cross-correlation by time aggregation.

3.4 Practical Issues

While the previous section discusses models and information shares, this section addresses the estimation of the model and related practical problems that arise.

3.4.1 Estimation

Although there are many ways to estimate the parameters of the system in Eq. (3.2), estimation is mostly straightforward. One complication is related to estimating $\mu = E(z_t)$. The first possibility is to calculate the sample average of the difference between the two prices, z_t. The equations can be estimated by OLS. We use an alternative procedure and estimate μ along with the other parameters applying seemingly unrelated regression (SUR). This has the additional advantage that we use all of the information contained in the covariance matrix of the innovations of the VECM.

The bondholder is paid the par value at the maturity date of a bond. Usually, bonds are also issued at a price close to the par value. Taking this feature into account, it is intuitive that the price of a bond does not follow a random walk in the long-run. However, the assumption that bond prices follow a random walk does hold in the short-run. Thus, the model is estimated separately for each day and these daily estimates are averaged for each bond.[92]

---

91 See Hasbrouck (1995), pp. 1182-1184, Baillie et al. (2002), pp. 314-316, Sapp (2002), pp. 428-429, and Hasbrouck (2003), p. 2383.

92 The same procedure is used by Hasbrouck (2003) for the analysis of the futures market and the corresponding underlying. See Hasbrouck (2003), p. 2386.

3.4.2 Choice of Price Variables

Surprisingly, we observe many negative inside spreads in the customer-dealer market.[93] A calculation of a midquote when the best bid-price is larger than the best ask-price is economically not reasonable. One possibility to circumvent this problem is the estimation of a VECM with four equations using bid- and ask-prices from both markets. Unfortunately, this procedure is computationally much more intense.[94] Therefore, we decided to estimate a VECM using bid-prices from both markets. A robustness check using a reduced sample has shown that the results for the VECM with ask-prices are qualitatively the same.

The set of bid-prices captures key summary data which any market participant might easily possess. Obviously, it is not comprehensive. Each of the markets produces information supplementary to the price and to the extent that this data is incrementally informative about future price movements, the information shares computed from a broader information set might differ from the present estimates.

Similarly, it is not clear whether our results for the EuroMTS system hold for the whole interdealer market, but since EuroMTS is one of the most important interdealer trading systems for government bond, the results provide valuable insight into the short-run dynamics between both market-spheres.

3.4.3 Nonsynchronous Prices

The specifications are estimated for time series in which t indexes intervals of wall-clock time which are five-second wide. When p_t is composed of the prices described in the preceding section, it will often include prices set prior to the start of interval t. As a result, p_t for t = 12:00:50 might include a bid-quote from the interdealer market first set at 12:00:05 and a bid-quote from the customer-dealer market first set at 12:00:20. Thus,

---

93 This phenomenon is also observed by other authors. See e.g. Garbade and Silber (1976), p 728. The authors provide five possible explanations for the disparity between dealer quotations: different inventory policies, heterogeneous expectations of future security prices, instability in supply-demand conditions, different cost of trading functions, and ignorance of other dealer quotes: See Garbade and Silber (1976), pp. 725-728.

94 In a VECM with 2 equations and 10 lags for each variable, 40 variables (plus error correction term) have to be estimated. In a VECM with 4 equations and 10 lags, 160 variables have to be estimated.

the prices represented by p_t were not set contemporaneously and are in a sense "stale" at t.

However, using the data on a very fine time scale has a major advantage for the calculation of the information shares. As emphasized in the previous section, the information share is not uniquely identified if the innovation covariance matrix is not diagonal. Suppose at 12:00:00, the best bid-price in the interdealer as well as the customer dealer market is 100. Now assume at 12:00:05, the bid price in the interdealer market changes to 101 and at 12:00:10, the bid-price in the customer dealer market changes to 101. These price changes would occur simultaneously on a 10-second basis. Therefore, time aggregation might introduce cross-correlation, and as a result, the upper and the lower bound of the information share diverge. The major drawback of time aggregation over long intervals is that it obscures short-term dynamics which are of major interest here.

3.4.4 Lag Lengths and Reducing the Number of Coefficients

The VECM specification (3.2) contains coefficient matrices B_i for each lag in the model. In other words, since each equation in the VECM contains all variables through all lags, the number of parameters is roughly Mn^2. When using a very fine time resolution, the number of coefficients is extremely large. If there are two prices, t indexes intervals of five seconds, and lagged terms up to five minutes are included, the number of coefficients in the model is roughly $2 \times 2 \times 60 = 240$. Some constraints are necessary to manage the dimensions of the estimation problem. As suggested by Hasbrouck (1995, 2003), we constrain the coefficients to lie on a polynomial function of the lag. For our data, 5 minutes of lagged prices are sufficient.[95] More exactly, we employ second-degree polynomial distributed lags over the lags 1-6, 7-12, 13-30 and 31-60.[96]

---

95 The determination of the lag length is based on residual diagnostics.

96 The use of polynomial distributed lags was first suggested by Almon (1965). See Almon (1965), pp. 180-181.

3.5 Data and Descriptive Statistics

The data were collected from Bloomberg L.P. over a period of 58 trading days between September 30, 2003 and December 19, 2003 for 118 government bonds issued by members of the EMU. To our knowledge, the 118 bonds correspond to all euro-denominated benchmark government bonds traded on EuroMTS at the beginning of the observation period.[97] Four bonds were deleted from the sample because of missing data in our records.

Table 3.1 provides an overview on the average bond characteristics of the 11 considered sovereign issuers. Overall, our sample consists of nonmissing data for 114 government bonds traded on EuroMTS during the whole observation period. The average time to maturity of our sample is 7.48 years on September 30, 2003. It varies between 5.69 years and 8.79 years depending on issuer. The next column presents the average age of the government bonds. It is defined as the time between the date of issue and the first day of our observation period. The average age of the EuroMTS traded bonds of the issuers in our sample is 2.21 years. The average amount outstanding is euro 11.60 billion where France has the largest issues with an average amount outstanding of euro 16.89 billion and Portugal having the smallest ones with euro 5.2 billion. Overall, our data comprises EMU government bonds with a total amount outstanding of euro 1,321.97 billion.

---

97 EuroMTS is an electronic trading system for Euro denominated benchmark government bonds. In 2003, benchmark government bonds of Austria, Belgium, Finland, France, Germany, Greece, Ireland, Italy, Portugal, the Netherlands, and Spain were available on the EuroMTS system. Quasi-sovereign and covered income bonds, which are also traded on EuroMTS, are not covered in this article. The eligible government bond universe includes bonds with an amount outstanding of euro 5 billion. The following maturity buckets have been selected for EuroMTS: (1.25-3.5 years), (3.5-6.5 years), (6.5-13.5 years), and (>13.5 years). Each bucket for each country is filled with the most recent issues until there are no more than 2 issues in the same year and no more than 3 bonds in each bucket.

Table 3.1: Bond Characteristics

This table provides an overview on the characteristics of the 114 bonds contained in our sample by issuer.

Issuer	No. of Bonds in Sample	Avg. Time to Maturity (years)	Avg. Age (years)	Avg. Amount Outstanding (billion euro)	Sum Amount Outstanding (billion euro)
AT	11	7.67	3.81	7.41	81.48
BE	9	8.79	2.96	10.47	94.23
DE	15	8.01	1.34	17.13	257.00
ES	13	7.51	2.34	10.95	142.30
FI	6	5.69	2.30	5.94	35.66
FR	13	7.66	1.88	16.80	218.42
GR	12	6.92	2.29	7.05	84.64
IR	3	8.73	2.57	6.86	20.59
IT	18	7.04	1.50	15.48	278.70
NL	7	8.67	1.88	10.36	72.52
PT	7	5.86	2.78	5.20	36.43
All	114	7.48	2.21	11.60	1,321.97

The data includes bid- and ask-quotes posted by a sample of 24 different dealers for the customer-dealer market as well as best bid- and best ask-prices for EuroMTS.[98] Table 3.2 exhibits all dealers included in our data. Quotations appearing on Bloomberg for the customer-dealer market are not firm, i.e., they may not be tradeable. One could argue that these quotes are better viewed as non-binding advertisements from the quoting dealers to attract customers, which do not contain any information. However, a counter argument to this criticism is the so-called reputation effect: Although quotes in the customer-dealer market are not technically firm, they may be seen as such, because dealers are forced to maintain a good record of quotations in order to build a good reputation as a liquidity provider. Posting quotes and refusing to trade at them is

98 The data were originally collected by alpha portfolio advisors GmbH to measure bond trading costs of institutional investors. The investors participating in this analysis were asked upfront which dealers provide reliable and continuous quotes for the bonds. The quotes disseminated by these dealers are comprised by our customer-dealer data. Since almost all banks provide quotes for the most liquid government bonds it is impossible to collect data on all dealers' quotes in the government bond market.

effectively precluded by the reputation effect.[99] The present study is not the only one relying on the assumption of the existence of the reputation effect. The assumption is also crucial for studies in the FX market analyzing triangular arbitrage,[100] trading intensity and volatility patterns in the spot market,[101] or the relationship between spreads and volatility[102].

Table 3.2: Bloomberg Contributors

This table provides an overview on the sources for the indicative quotes in the customer-dealer market. Quotes were collected for 24 different dealers from Bloomberg L.P. over the sample period of 58 trading days between September 30, 2003 and December 19, 2003.

Contributor		Name	Contributor		Name
1	ABN	ABN Amro Bank	13	HSET	HSBC Execution
2	BARX	Barclays Capital	14	HVBT	HVB E-Bond Trade
3	BAYL	Bayerische Landesbank	15	JPEX	JPMorgan Auto-Ex
4	BPGL	BNP Paribas	16	JPM	JP Morgan WM
5	CBKF	Commerzbank Financial	17	LBEX	Lehman Brothers
6	CSEG	CSFB London	18	MLIL	Merrill Lynch Intl.
7	DAB	Deutsche Bank Autobahn	19	MSEG	Morgan Stanley London
8	DAVY	Davy Dublin	20	NDEA	Nordea Bank
9	DRET	Dresdner Bank ET	21	RBCL	RBC Dominion London
10	DRKW	Dresdner Kleinwort	22	SB	Citigroup Autoexec
11	DZAG	DZ Bank	23	WDRL	UBS London
12	GDSB	Allied Irish Bank	24	WLBG	West LB

We filter the quote data to eliminate obvious errors. In detail, we eliminate a quote if a dealer's bid-price is larger than his ask-price. Additionally, we delete price jumps and reversals of more than 1.5%. Since we cannot observe whether a dealer's unchanged quotes keep valid or are already obsolete, quotes are assumed to be valid until the dealer posts a new quote. If the dealer doesn't post a new quote within 5

[99] See Bollerslev and Domowitz (1993), p. 1422.
[100] See, e.g., de Jong, Mahieu, and Schotman (1998).
[101] See, e.g., Bollerslev and Domowitz (1993), and Dacorogna et al. (1993).
[102] See, e.g., Bollerslev and Melvin (1994).

minutes, we set this dealer's quotes to missing. We define the best bid-quote as the largest valid bid-quote across all dealers at a certain point of time and the best ask-quote as the lowest ask-price respectively.

Collecting the entire data – the EuroMTS interdealer-data as well as the indicative quotes for the customer-dealer market – from the same source (Bloomberg) has one major advantage: We do not have to worry about time stamps. If the data were collected from different sources (e.g. Bloomberg for the customer-dealer market and MTS for the interdealer data) non-synchronous reporting of time stamps might lead to timing errors. Although market participants generally attempt accurate system clocks, data collected from different systems might not replicate the real-time public market data stream as our data does.

An overview on the quote data can be found in Table 3.3. In the customer-dealer market, our data contains on average 1.19 million quotes per bond (or 135.66 million quotes for all bonds). At the 5th percentile, we still observe about 401,770 quotes per bond. In terms of best bid-quotes, we observe – using the above outlined methodology to determine the prevailing best bid-price – on average about 159,950 bid-prices in the customer-dealer market. The best bid-quote changes on average less frequently in the interdealer market with 132,750 observed adjusted quotes. Nevertheless, the difference in the number of quotes between the two markets is not very large. This avoids the problem of systematically retaining obsolete quotes for one of the two markets. On average, the dealers post their quotes with a spread of 6.15 bp in the customer-dealer market. The quoted spread varies strongly across the different issues. While we observe a spread of only 3.34 bp at the 5th percentile, the quoted spread is about 15.93 bp at the 95th percentile. The variation in the spread may be attributed to differences in issuer, time to maturity, credit rating, age, and amount outstanding.[103] In fact, we find evidence that, in our sample, the average spread increases with the time to maturity of a bond. The average quoted inside spread of 1.03 basis points for the customer dealer market has to be interpreted with caution. The next column shows the percentage of crossed or locked inside quotes.[104] The sample average of 21.73 % is very high.[105] The average

[103] An overview on the costs of trading bonds and the variables influencing trading costs can be found in Hong and Warga (2000), Schultz (2001), Chakravarty and Sarkar (2003), Edwards, Harris, and Piwowar (2004), Bessembinder, Maxwell, and Venkataraman (2005), and Part 4 of this dissertation.

[104] The term crossed refers to inside quotes where the best bid-quote is larger than the best ask-quote, while locked quotes are quotes where the best bid-quote equals the best ask-quote.

quoted spread increases to 1.81 bp after deleting the economically not interpretable crossed and locked quotes. The last column of Table 3.3 exhibits the quoted inside spreads in the interdealer market by issuer. With an average of 5.18 bp they are very similar to the individual dealers quoted spread of 6.15 bp, but much larger than the inside spread posted in the customer-dealer market of 1.81 bp. The intransparency of the customer-dealer market obviously leads to a much smaller inside spread in the customer-dealer market than in the interdealer market. Possible reasons for a large dispersion in the quotes are listed in Garbade and Silber (1976).[106] Finally, Figure 3.1 plots one day of data for a German federal security with ISIN DE0001135200 in 5-second intervals. With a time to maturity of 8.78 years at the first day of our observation period, it is presumably a very liquid bond, since it was deliverable in the Bund future contract at this time. The large amount outstanding of euro 27 billion also indicates that this issue is very liquid. Only quotes during regular EuroMTS market hours from 8:15am to 5:30pm are used in the analysis.

3.6 Price Discovery in European Government Bond Markets

The price set modeled for the bond data consists of the best bid-quote prevailing at the end of each 5-second interval for both the interdealer and the customer dealer market. The specification in Eq. (3.2) is estimated with 5 minutes of lags. The parameter estimations of the VECM are difficult to interpret, and not reported for the sake of brevity. Before considering the information share estimations for all 114 bonds covered by the data, it is useful to examine the results of the estimated system for one bond.

---

[105] Cao, Ghysels, and Hatheway (2000) analyze the price discovery during the NASDAQ preopening. On NASDAQ, during the preopening, individual market makers' indicative quotes are displayed and widely disseminated in the absence of trading. They find 34.9% of the quotes during the preopening at Nasdaq are either crosses or locks. The frequency drops to 4.2% during the first five minutes following the market opening and to virtually zero during the rest of the trading day. See Cao, Ghysels and Hatheway (2000), p. 1347.

[106] See Garbade and Silber (1976), pp. 725-728.

Table 3.3: Descriptive Data

This table provides the descriptive statistics for the quotes collected from Bloomberg for both the customer-dealer as well as the interdealer market. The quotes for the customer-dealer market are indicative, while the quotes for the interdealer market are tradeable. The reported mean is an average over 114 government bonds traded on EuroMTS during the observation period. All spreads as well as the percentage of crossed and locked quotes are time-weighted. P5, P25, P50, P75, and P95 denote the 5th, 25th, 50th, 75th, and 95th percentile respectively.

	Customer-Dealer						EuroMTS	
	Avg. No. of Bids per Bond (000s)	**Avg. No. of Inside Quote Revisions per Bond (000s)**	**Avg. Quoted Spread (bp)**	**Avg. Quoted Inside Spread (bp)**	**Crossed and Locked Quotes (%)**	**Avg. Quoted Inside Spread w/o Negative (bp)**	**Avg. Nr. of Bids per Bond (000s)**	**Avg. Quoted Inside Spread (bp)**
Mean	1,187.13	159.95	6.15	1.03	21.73	1.81	132.75	5.18
Std	*468.46*	*72.17*	*3.78*	*1.22*	*12.69*	*1.49*	*49.63*	*4.60*
P5	401.77	53.73	3.34	-0.31	4.91	0.81	54.04	2.19
P25	788.63	84.53	4.10	0.42	12.41	1.04	84.41	2.78
P50	1,274.97	178.11	4.74	0.75	19.72	1.22	140.55	3.30
P75	1,576.55	226.41	6.03	1.31	28.22	1.78	168.22	4.87
P95	1,786.66	252.81	15.93	3.60	47.93	6.19	204.99	16.92

Figure 3.1: One Day of Data

This figure plots one day of data for a German Federal security with ISIN DE0001135200 in 5-second intervals. The bond has a maturity of 8.78 years at the first day of our observation period and an amount outstanding of euro 27 billion.

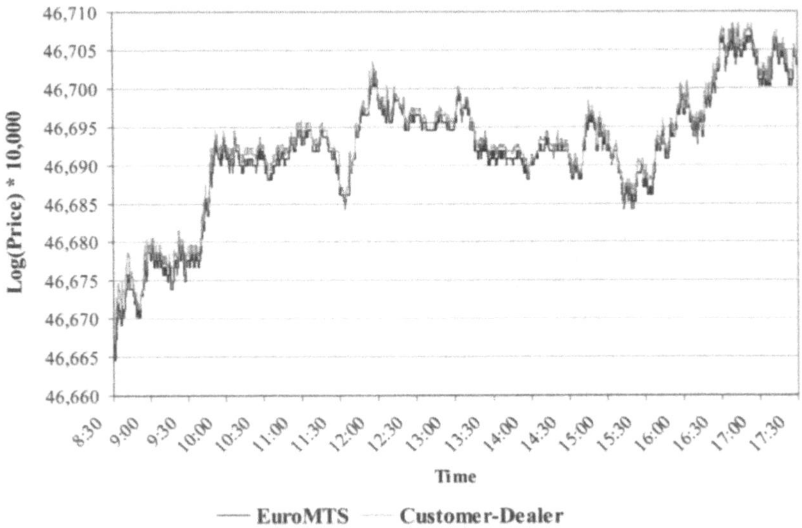

Figure 3.2 depicts the impulse response function for one German government bond, i.e. the cumulative price impacts implied by an initial 1-unit shock to the interdealer market bid-price. The two lines track the implied cumulative price changes for the interdealer and the customer-dealer market. By construction, in t=0, the impact is unity in the EuroMTS bid-price, and zero in the best customer-dealer bid price. In the long run, the impact has to be essentially the same for both prices. Otherwise, long-term arbitrage possibilities prevail. This is the case after approximately 40 minutes. The initial shock to the EuroMTS bid-quote quickly dies out with only a small persistent impact on the best bid-quote in the customer dealer market. Therefore, the largest part of the price impact implied by a shock to the interdealer bid-price is of transitory nature.

Figure 3.2: Impulse Response Function to a One-Unit Shock in the Interdealer Market

This figure shows the impulse response function for the bid-prices in the customer-dealer and the interdealer market to a one unit shock in the interdealer market. The estimates are based on a vector error correction model of the two price series of a German federal security with ISIN DE0001135200 estimated at a 5-second resolution.

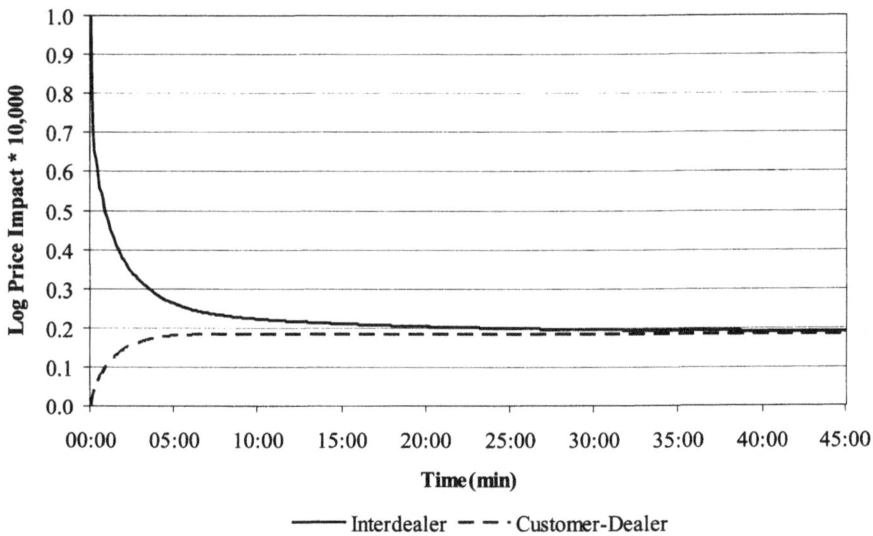

Figure 3.3 exhibits the impulse response function to a shock in the best bid-price of the customer-dealer market. The permanent part of the price impact in the customer-dealer market dies out within a few minutes. The EuroMTS price takes much longer to adjust to the new long-run equilibrium reached after about 35 minutes than the price in the customer-dealer market. The permanent component of the price impact after a shock to the customer-dealer bid-quote is about 70%. This is high compared to the 20% permanent component of a shock to the interdealer market.

Figure 3.3: Impulse Response Function to a One-Unit Shock in the Customer-Dealer Market

This figure shows the impulse response function for the bid-prices in the customer-dealer and the interdealer market to a one unit shock in the customer-dealer market. The estimates are based on a vector error correction model of the two price series of a German federal security with ISIN DE0001135200 estimated at a 5-second resolution.

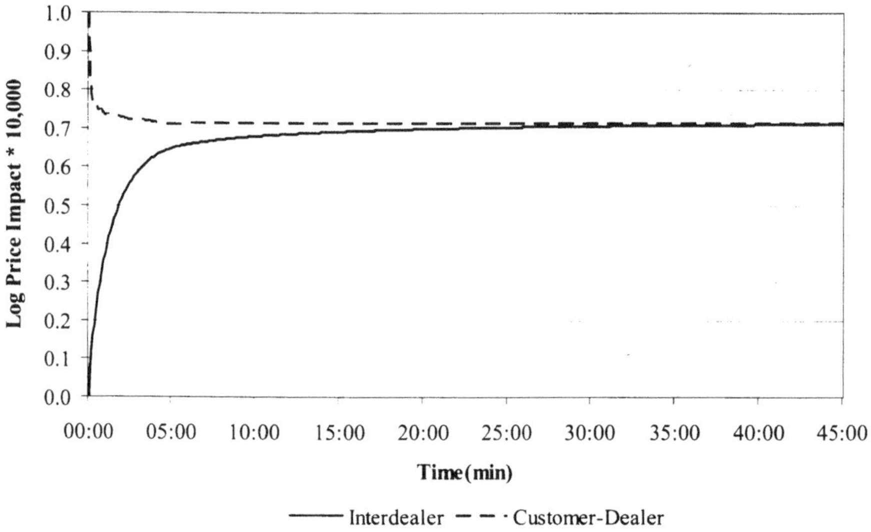

Table 3.4 presents the estimation results relating to the information shares of this particular bond. The correlation refers to the cross-correlation of the innovations ε_t in the VECM in Eq. (3.2). The smaller the cross-correlation, the smaller the difference between the upper bound (Infoshare Max) and the lower bound (Infoshare Min) of the information share of a market. A correlation of about 0.24 indicates that the difference between the upper and the lower bound of the information share is presumably large. The strong cross-correlation of the residuals in the VECM for this bond can be attributed (at least partially) to the high liquidity and the high quote intensity of this bond.[107] The next two columns exhibit the coefficients of the efficient price. They are directly derived from the impulse response functions in Figures 3.2 and 3.3. The coefficients of the efficient price represent the long-run

[107] For an explanation see Section 3.4.3.

Table 3.4: Price Discovery in an Exemplary Bond

The statistics in this table are based on a vector error correction model of interdealer and customer-dealer bid-prices for a German federal security with ISIN DE0001135200 estimated at a 5-second resolution. The quotes for the customer-dealer market are indicative while the interdealer-quotes are tradable quotes. The model is estimated for 58 trading days between September 30, 2003 and December 19, 2003.

			Coefficients of the Efficient Price		EuroMTS (p1)		Customer-Dealer (p2)	
Issuer	**ISIN**	**Correlation**	**EuroMTS**	**Customer-Dealer**	**Infoshare Max**	**Infoshare Min**	**Infoshare Max**	**Infoshare Min**
DE	DE0001135200	0.2430	0.1905	0.7107	0.2679	0.1076	0.8924	0.7321

best-bid quote respectively. In other words, the coefficients of the efficient price equal $\psi = (\psi_1, \psi_2)$, one of the identical rows of the impact matrix $\Psi(1)$ in Eq. (3.8). The next columns present the upper and the lower bound of the information share for both markets. The upper and lower bound is 26.79% and 10.76% for the interdealer market. Thelike figures for the customer-dealer market are 89.24% and 73.21%. For this bond, the customer-dealer market is by far the more dominant market, accounting for roughly 80% of the price discovery. This result does not confirm our Hypothesis H1. However, we cannot draw a final conclusion from one bond, especially since the bond chosen for the analysis is very liquid.

Table 3.5 reports sample means, standard deviations, medians and different percentiles of the information shares and estimates relating to the information shares for all 114 bonds covered by the data. The second column describes the off-diagonal correlations. They are on average 0.1664 and, therefore, smaller than for the bond analyzed in the last paragraph. The median is roughly the same. The next two columns present the coefficients of the efficient price. The average coefficient for the customer-dealer market is 0.5123, while the average coefficient for EuroMTS is only 0.2660. Although the small permanent component of the price impact in the interdealer market is surprising, it is in line with the results of the bond analyzed above. The percentiles show that the variation across bonds in the coefficients is large. At the 95th percentile, the EuroMTS-coefficient is 0.6293. Therefore, the permanent component of a shock in the EuroMTS market is relatively large at least for some of the bonds in our sample.

Table 3.5: Price Discovery in Multiple-Dealership Markets

The statistics in this table are based on a vector error correction model of interdealer and customer-dealer bid-prices for 114 government bonds traded on EuroMTS. The VECM is estimated at a 5-second resolution. The quotes for the customer-dealer market are indicative while the interdealer-quotes are tradable quotes. The model is estimated for 58 trading days between September 30, 2003 and December 19, 2003. The table shows equal weighted averages and corresponding summary statistics.

		Coefficients of the Efficient Price		EuroMTS (p1)		Customer-Dealer (p2)	
	Correlation	**EuroMTS**	**Customer-Dealer**	**Infoshare Max**	**Infoshare Min**	**Infoshare Max**	**Infoshare Min**
Mean	0.1664	0.2660	0.5123	0.2790	0.1746	0.8254	0.7210
Std	*0.0683*	*0.1686*	*0.2064*	*0.1210*	*0.1348*	*0.1348*	*0.1208*
P5	0.0484	0.0001	0.1574	0.1394	0.0407	0.5295	0.4825
P25	0.1179	0.1605	0.3520	0.1838	0.0706	0.7633	0.6432
Med	0.1686	0.2450	0.5487	0.2486	0.1249	0.8751	0.7514
P75	0.2249	0.3389	0.6661	0.3568	0.2367	0.9294	0.8162
P95	0.2737	0.6293	0.7845	0.5175	0.4705	0.9593	0.8606

The next two columns exhibit the statistics for the upper and lower bound of the information share for the interdealer market. The average upper bound of the information share is 27.90% and the average lower bound of the information share is 17.46%. The average upper and lower bound of the information share for the customer dealer market is 82.54% and 72.10% respectively. Although the variation across bonds is large, the results show that the customer-dealer market is by far the more dominant of the two markets. The results for both markets at the 95th percentile show that the interdealer market's information share is only for a few bonds larger than 50%. The share of the interdealer market in the price discovery process is surprisingly small. Because of its relatively high transparency and stronger concentration, we would have expected a much higher information share for the interdealer market. Based on our sample of very liquid euro-denominated government bonds, we cannot confirm our first hypothesis H1. The results contradict the hypothesis that the impounding of order flow information in the interdealer market results in a lead of this market over the customer-dealer market, which is supported by Lyons (2001) for the FX market.[108] Although not dominant, the interdealer market's contribution to the efficient bond price is (economically) significant for most of the bonds. Variations in the information share, however, might be due to differences in liquidity of the bonds. The relationship between bond characteristics/liquidity and a market's information share is the focus of the next section.

Although our results are surprising given the differences in transparency and trading mechanisms of the two markets, they support the findings of the information processing literature that indicative quotes do contain information. Biais, Hillion and Spatt (1999) examine the price discovery and learning process during the preopening period in the Paris Bourse. More exactly, they test the hypothesis that indicative prices are noise against the hypothesis that nonbinding prices during preopening reflect learning. They cannot reject the noise hypothesis early in the preopening. As the opening gets closer, the informational content and efficiency of prices increase and the learning hypothesis is not rejected. Cao, Ghysels and Hatheway (2000) find evidence that dealers use crossed and locked quotes during the preopening at NASDAQ to convey information on the efficient price. Periods with locked or crossed quotes

[108] See Lyons (2001), p. 115.

contribute more to the price discovery process than periods with positive quoted spreads.

3.7 Price Discovery and Liquidity

The results in the last section showed a large variation across the different securities contained in the sample of 114 government bonds. The discussion on the efficiency of open outcry versus electronic trading mechanisms outlined in Section 3.1 revealed some interesting insights. During periods with high volatility and trading intensity, the open outcry system contributed more to the price discovery than in periods with low volatility.[109] If the importance of a market for the price discovery varies over time with the market conditions, we should also observe a relation between price contribution and security characteristics as suggested by Hypothesis H2. For bonds, we expect a negative relationship between the EuroMTS information shares and the liquidity of a bond. We use the following bond-related proxies to measure the liquidity of a bond:

Time to maturity: The maturity of a bond proxies its interest rate exposure. Bonds which mature later have a higher interest rate exposure. Keeping all other factors constant, they are usually more expensive to trade and, therefore, less liquid.[110]

Age: The age of a bond is defined as the time between issuance date and the first day of the observation period. It is well known that many bond investors like large insurance companies are buy-and-hold investors. A large fraction of the issue is absorbed in the portfolios of those investors, reducing the liquidity of the bond.[111]

Amount outstanding: Garbade and Silber (1976) show that the amount outstanding is negatively related to a dealer's quoted bid-ask spread. A larger amount

---

109 This question is not analyzed for two reasons. Firstly, extensive research already exists on this issue. Secondly, our data contains 58 trading days. The observation period is too short to categorize the trading days into periods with low high and normal volatility. Additionally, results may be biased if the average volatility during this period deviates strongly from the long-term average.

110 See, e.g., Hong and Warga (2000), p. 38, Chakravarty and Sarkar (2003), p. 43, and Edwards, Harris, and Piwowar (2004), p. 7.

111 See, e.g., Sarig and Warga (1989), pp. 369-370, Amihud and Mendelson (1991), p. 1413, Chakravarty and Sarkar (2003), p. 43.

outstanding results in a larger quantity potentially available for trade and therefore higher marketability.[112]

In addition to the bond characteristics, we also use market-related liquidity variables. They have a major advantage over the bond-related characteristics. Imagine a German federal security with 9 years time to maturity and assume a small amount was issued a long time ago. Despite the bond characteristics indicating a very illiquid bond, it is probably very liquid. The reason is that the bond is deliverable in the Bund future contract. Hence, all investors with a position in the Bund future are interested in the price of the bond and the trading volume of this bond is presumably very high as long as it is deliverable. This relationship is not covered by bond-related liquidity characteristics alone, but may be conveyed by market related liquidity proxies. The following market-related proxies are used in our analysis.

Number of quotes: Dealers are more active in liquid bonds since their customers especially expect them to post continuously up-to-date prices in these instruments.

Quoted spread: Intuitively, the quoted spread of a very liquid bond is smaller than the quoted spread of an illiquid bond.

Percentage of time-weighted non-positive customer-dealer inside quotes: Garbade and Silber (1976) argue that the probability of a crossed quote decreases with trading volume, because market participants will uncover this arbitrage opportunity faster.[113] Therefore, we expect bonds with a larger percentage of time-weighted negative quotes to be less liquid.

---

112 See, among others, Garbade and Silber (1976), p. 739.

113 See Garbade and Silber (1976), p. 728.

Table 3.6: Price Discovery and Security-Related Liquidity Characteristics

The statistics in this table are based on a vector error correction model of interdealer and customer-dealer bid-prices for 114 government bonds traded on EuroMTS. The VECM is estimated at a 5-second resolution. The quotes for the customer-dealer market are indicative while the interdealer-quotes are tradeable. The model is estimated for 58 trading days between September 30, 2003 and December 19, 2003. The data on the 114 bonds is divided into quintiles. The table shows equal weighted averages and corresponding summary statistics for each quintile. Panel A shows the results by quintiles of the time to maturity, Panel B by quintiles of the age and Panel C by quintiles of the amount outstanding.

Panel A: Time to Maturity

			Coefficients of the Efficient Price		EuroMTS (p1)		Customer-Dealer (p2)	
Quintile	**Avg. Time to Maturity (years)**	**Correlation**	**EuroMTS**	**Customer-Dealer**	**Infoshare Max**	**Infoshare Min**	**Infoshare Max**	**Infoshare Min**
1	1.7409	0.0799	0.3671	0.3186	0.3777	0.3208	0.6792	0.6223
2	3.2896	0.1417	0.3034	0.3822	0.2346	0.1453	0.8547	0.7654
3	5.6501	0.2078	0.2445	0.5750	0.2579	0.1295	0.8705	0.7421
4	8.8187	0.2306	0.2337	0.6183	0.2740	0.1283	0.8717	0.7260
5	17.8151	0.1740	0.1802	0.6700	0.2498	0.1472	0.8528	0.7502

Panel B: Age

Quintile	Avg. Age (years)	Correlation	Coefficients of the Efficient Price		EuroMTS (p1)		Customer-Dealer (p2)	
			EuroMTS	Customer-Dealer	Infoshare Max	Infoshare Min	Infoshare Max	Infoshare Min
1	0.4772	0.1755	0.2286	0.5301	0.2671	0.1586	0.8414	0.7329
2	1.1499	0.1741	0.2345	0.5740	0.2493	0.1456	0.8544	0.7507
3	1.8052	0.1770	0.2988	0.5066	0.2714	0.1625	0.8375	0.7286
4	2.7409	0.1463	0.3100	0.4609	0.3156	0.2135	0.7865	0.6844
5	4.8673	0.1598	0.2593	0.4896	0.2912	0.1923	0.8077	0.7088

Panel C: Amount Outstanding

Quintile	Avg. Amount Outstanding (billion euro)	Correlation	Coefficients of the Efficient Price		EuroMTS (p1)		Customer-Dealer (p2)	
			EuroMTS	Customer-Dealer	Infoshare Max	Infoshare Min	Infoshare Max	Infoshare Min
1	5.7373	0.1976	0.2223	0.5390	0.2371	0.1212	0.8788	0.7629
2	7.8219	0.1827	0.2084	0.6032	0.2478	0.1384	0.8616	0.7522
3	10.9495	0.1350	0.3609	0.3992	0.3460	0.2541	0.7459	0.6540
4	13.7844	0.1412	0.2766	0.4913	0.3106	0.2157	0.7843	0.6894
5	19.6602	0.1743	0.2659	0.5239	0.2563	0.1471	0.8529	0.7437

Table 3.6 reports information shares and relating estimates by security characteristics. The results are reported for all quintiles of the relevant variable. Panel A exhibits the results by maturity, Panel B by age and Panel C by amount outstanding. The information shares of the interdealer market in the shortest maturity quintile are the largest with an upper bound of 37.77% and a lower bound of 32.08%. Although EuroMTS has the largest information share in the quintile with the shortest maturity, the relationship between amount outstanding and information share of EuroMTS is not linear. We observe the lowest information shares in the second quintile. The EuroMTS information shares in the quintiles three through five are slightly higher and roughly the same. Since information shares have to sum up to one, the maximum information share in the customer-dealer market equals (1 – minimum information share interdealer market). The information shares for different age and amount outstanding quintiles behave very similarly. Based on the univariate analysis, we cannot find a clear relationship between bond related-market characteristics and the contribution of a market to the price discovery process.

Table 3.7 exhibits the information shares by quintiles of the market-related liquidity measures. Panel A and B relate the information shares to the number of new quotes observed during the observation period in the interdealer and the customer-dealer market respectively. For the number of quote changes in both markets, the lowest quintile exhibits the largest EuroMTS information share. The interdealer market's contribution to the price discovery is larger for bonds with fewer quotes. This supports our hypothesis H2 that the interdealer market with its tradable quotes contributes more to the price discovery for illiquid bonds than for liquid bonds. The relationship between the number of quote changes in EuroMTS and the information shares of both markets is not linear. The average EuroMTS information share is the smallest for the bonds in the third quintiles, while it increases again in the fourth and fifth quintile. The results of Panel B, on the other hand, strengthen the hypothesized relationship in H2. We observe the largest average EuroMTS information share for the bonds in quintile one and the smallest average EuroMTS information share for the bonds in quintile five.

Table 3.7: Price Discovery and Market Related Liquidity Characteristics

The statistics in this table are based on a vector error correction model of interdealer and customer-dealer bid-prices for 114 government bonds traded on EuroMTS. The VECM is estimated at a 5-second resolution. The quotes for the customer-dealer market are indicative while the interdealer-quotes are tradeable. The model is estimated for 58 trading days between September 30, 2003 and December 19, 2003. The data on the 114 bonds is divided into quintiles. The table shows equal weighted averages and corresponding summary statistics for each quintile. Panel A shows the results by quintiles of the number of changes of the inside quote in EuroMTS, Panel B by quintiles of the number of changes of the inside quotes in the customer-dealer market, Panel C by quintiles of the time-weighted quoted spread in EuroMTS, Panel D by quintiles of the dealers' average time-weighted quoted spread, and Panel E by quintiles of the percentage of crossed and locked quotes in the customer-dealer market (time-weighted).

Panel A: Number of quote changes in EuroMTS

			Coefficients of the Efficient Price		EuroMTS (p1)		Customer-Dealer (p2)	
Quintile	No. of Quote Changes EuroMTS	Correlation	EuroMTS	Customer-Dealer	Infoshare Max	Infoshare Min	Infoshare Max	Infoshare Min
1	58,746	0.0919	0.3342	0.3251	0.3558	0.2919	0.7081	0.6442
2	103,410	0.1395	0.3121	0.4282	0.2395	0.1563	0.8437	0.7605
3	141,664	0.1946	0.1833	0.6352	0.2243	0.1091	0.8909	0.7757
4	164,573	0.1949	0.2322	0.6082	0.2546	0.1339	0.8661	0.7454
5	195,735	0.2126	0.2644	0.5700	0.3182	0.1791	0.8209	0.6818

Panel B: Number of quote changes in the customer-dealer (B2C) market

			Coefficients of the Efficient Price		EuroMTS (p1)		Customer-Dealer (p2)	
Quintile	No. of Quote Changes B2C	Correlation	EuroMTS	Customer-Dealer	Infoshare Max	Infoshare Min	Infoshare Max	Infoshare Min
1	58,827	0.0841	0.3701	0.2999	0.3636	0.3055	0.6945	0.6364
2	103,495	0.1485	0.3039	0.4047	0.2693	0.1718	0.8282	0.7307
3	171,756	0.1624	0.2548	0.5539	0.2797	0.1792	0.8208	0.7203
4	219,483	0.2123	0.2450	0.5968	0.2792	0.1395	0.8605	0.7208
5	246,694	0.2247	0.1556	0.7079	0.2031	0.0773	0.9227	0.7969

Panel C: Time-weighted average quoted spread on EuroMTS

			Coefficients of the Efficient Price		EuroMTS (p1)		Customer-Dealer (p2)	
Quintile	Spread EMTS	Correlation	EuroMTS	Customer-Dealer	Infoshare Max	Infoshare Min	Infoshare Max	Infoshare Min
1	2.2970	0.1018	0.3626	0.3276	0.3442	0.2757	0.7243	0.6558
2	2.8544	0.1587	0.2606	0.4912	0.2986	0.1938	0.8062	0.7014
3	3.3399	0.1930	0.2803	0.4850	0.2658	0.1446	0.8554	0.7342
4	4.6338	0.2154	0.2324	0.5891	0.2315	0.1060	0.8940	0.7685
5	12.7117	0.1645	0.1945	0.6674	0.2542	0.1516	0.8484	0.7458

Panel D: Time-weighted average quoted spread in the customer-dealer (B2C) market

			Coefficients of the Efficient Price		EuroMTS (p1)		Customer-Dealer (p2)	
Quintile	Avg. Spread B2C	Correlation	EuroMTS	Customer-Dealer	Infoshare Max	Infoshare Min	Infoshare Max	Infoshare Min
1	3.4939	0.1268	0.3351	0.4090	0.3046	0.2271	0.7729	0.6954
2	4.2408	0.1539	0.3040	0.4475	0.2919	0.1882	0.8118	0.7081
3	4.7573	0.1845	0.2686	0.5103	0.2849	0.1631	0.8369	0.7151
4	5.6634	0.1924	0.2489	0.5188	0.2708	0.1529	0.8471	0.7292
5	12.5476	0.1755	0.1733	0.6758	0.2429	0.1412	0.8588	0.7571

Panel E: Percentage of crossed and locked quotes

			Coefficients of the Efficient Price		EuroMTS (p1)		Customer-Dealer (p2)	
Quintile	Percentage Cross/Lock	Correlation	EuroMTS	Customer-Dealer	Infoshare Max	Infoshare Min	Infoshare Max	Infoshare Min
1	7.3259	0.2032	0.1462	0.6511	0.2054	0.0890	0.9110	0.7946
2	14.0666	0.2018	0.2325	0.5876	0.1952	0.0789	0.9211	0.8048
3	19.5489	0.1273	0.3424	0.4037	0.3156	0.2324	0.7676	0.6844
4	25.6987	0.1501	0.3043	0.4567	0.3223	0.2199	0.7801	0.6777
5	41.9033	0.1482	0.3077	0.4577	0.3580	0.2554	0.7446	0.6420

Panel C reports the information shares of both markets by quintiles of the inside spread in the interdealer market. The bonds in the lowest quintile have the lowest average quoted spreads in the sample and are thereby the most liquid instruments. Surprisingly, the prices on EuroMTS are more informative for more liquid bonds than for less liquid bonds. The EuroMTS information share is largest in the first quintile and is lowest in the fifth, third through fifth quintile. But still, the customer-dealer market remains more dominant for all quintiles. Panel D uses the average quoted spread in the customer-dealer market posted by individual dealers as liquidity proxy. Again, the interdealer market is more important for liquid securities than for illiquid securities. In this panel the information share of EuroMTS decreases from the first through the fifth quintile. The results based on Panel C and Panel D contradict our hypothesis H2, that the share of EuroMTS in the price discovery process is larger for less liquid bonds.

Panel E relates the time-weighted percentage of crossed and locked quotes in the customer-dealer market to the information share of both markets. The customer dealer market is by far more dominant for the bonds in the first two quintiles (the quintiles where the percentage of negative quotes is lowest) compared to the bonds in quintiles three to five. The results from Panel E therefore support the hypothesis H2 since, as explained above, a higher percentage of negative quotes is usually observed for more illiquid bonds.

To capture the interrelation of the liquidity-related variables in Table 3.6 and the market related variables in Table 3.7, we estimate a cross section regression using the liquidity proxies as explanatory variables and the bonds' information shares of EuroMTS as dependent variable. The test statistics were calculated using White's (1980) heteroscedasticity consistent covariance matrix. The dependent variable is the bonds' lower bound of the EuroMTS information share. Different liquidity proxies are used as explanatory variables in the four models. We do not include the same variables calculated from the data of both markets (e.g. number of quote changes in EuroMTS and number of quote changes in the customer-dealer market) into the same regression model, because these variables are highly correlated. Moreover, the time to maturity is strongly correlated to the quoted spread in both markets. The correlation coefficient of about 0.89 is very high taking into account the small sample of 114 observations.[114] To avoid the problems arising from multicolinearity, we account either for time to maturity, or for the number of quotes, but not for both variables at the same time in the different specifications of our regression model. Coefficients at least significant at a 10% significance level are exhibited in bold letters. The first two models use data from EuroMTS for the number of observed quote changes and the average quoted spread, whereas time to maturity is included into the first model and the quoted spread on EuroMTS is included into the second model. None of the bond-related liquidity characteristics, age, time to maturity and amount outstanding, have a significant effect on the information share of a bond on EuroMTS. The coefficients for these variables are insignificant in the first two model specifications. The number of inside quote changes per bond is significant on a 1%-level in model (I) as well as model (II). The sign of the coefficient is the same in both specifications. The bonds' EuroMTS information share is negatively related to the number of quote changes on EuroMTS. Since we expect to observe more dealers quoting with a higher frequency for more liquid bonds, this finding is in line with our second hypothesis H2. The average quoted spread is included as an explanatory variable only in the second model. The coefficient is insignificant and the existence of a systematic relationship between the quoted spread and the EuroMTS information share cannot be confirmed. This is surprising, since the quoted spread is one of the most obvious liquidity variables representing the dealers' view of a security's liquidity. The last variable, the time-weighted proportion of the crossed or locked quotes is significant at the 1%-level. The impact on the information share is positive. That means, the higher the percentage of crossed or locked quotes in a bond, the higher the information share of EuroMTS. This again confirms our hypothesis H2. The estimation of the specifications in columns (III) and (IV) where the number of quote changes, as well as the quoted spread is calculated from the data for the customer-dealer market, confirms the results from the first two columns. Additionally the time to maturity is significant in the model of column (III) and the average quoted spread by dealers in the customer-dealer market is significant in column (IV). The signs of the coefficients are in line with our expectations and once more confirm hypothesis H2. The adjusted R-squared of our regression is between 39% and 50% through all four specifications of the regression model. The liquidity proxies used in our analysis thus explain between 39% and 50% of the cross sectional variation in the information shares.

---

[114] The correlation is almost independent of the market used to determine the number of quote changes.

F-values were computed to test the joint significance of the explanatory variables. They are significant at a 1%-level for all specifications. Adjusted R-squared and F-statistics confirm that the fit of our model is very good.

Table 3.8: Regression Results

This table exhibits the results of a cross section regression of each bond's lower bound of the EuroMTS information share on different bond and market-related liquidity variables. Spreads as well as the proportion of crossed/locked quotes are determined on a time-weighted basis. Significant coefficients are exhibited in bold letters and *p*-values are reported below each coefficient. The standard errors used to calculate the t-statistics are obtained using White (1980)'s heteroscedasticity-consistent covariance matrix.

Dependent Variable	**Information Share EuroMTS Lower Bound**			
	(I)	(II)	(III)	(IV)
Const	**0.1834**	**0.1712**	**0.2073**	**0.1680**
	0.0001	*0.0002*	*0.0000*	*0.0000*
Age	0.0078	0.0079	0.0056	0.0049
	0.1965	*0.1980*	*0.2943*	*0.3849*
Time to Maturity	0.0028		**0.0052**	
	0.2073		*0.0002*	
Amount Outstanding	-0.0002	-0.0002	0.0013	0.0023
	0.8925	*0.9252*	*0.3517*	*0.1260*
No. of EuroMTS Quotes (000s)	**-0.0012**	**-0.0011**		
	0.0000	*0.0000*		
No. of Customer-Dealer Inside Quotes			**-0.0012**	**-0.0010**
			0.0000	*0.0000*
EuroMTS Spread		0.0027		
		0.3089		
Customer-Dealer Spread				**0.0069**
				0.0096
Proportion of Crosses and Locks (Time Weighted)	**0.5837**	**0.5869**	**0.4312**	**0.4442**
	0.0000	*0.0000*	*0.0000*	*0.0000*
Adjusted R^2	0.3963	0.3900	0.4997	0.4844
F-statistic	11.2281	11.2893	21.9454	19.4276
Prob(F-statistic)	0.0001	0.0000	0.0000	0.0000
N	114	114	114	114

A graphical test for the economic significance of the variables is shown in Figure 3.4. The lower bounds of the EuroMTS information share is plotted against different values of the number of quotes in EuroMTS and the proportion of crossed and locked quotes based on the regression results of the first model specification in Table 3.8. A fitted lower bound of the information share of 0.5280 is obtained for a bond with 20,000 quotes and a high proportion of crossed and locked quotes of 57%. The EuroMTS information share clearly rises with the proportion of crossed and locked quotes and decreases with an increasing number of observed quotes. The strong variation of the information share confirms the economic significance of the market related liquidity proxies. In our sample however, keeping all other factors constant, the information share of EuroMTS is only larger than 0.5 for bonds with a very large proportion of locked/crossed quotes (approximately larger than 53%) and a very small number of quote changes (smaller than 40,000 quotes).

Although not all of the liquidity proxies are significant in our regression model, some of them are related to the EuroMTS information share of a bond. For the significant liquidity proxies, we find the expected signs. Especially the number of quote changes, which is a proxy for the dealer activity in a certain bond, and the percentage of crossed and locked quotes proved to have a significant impact on the information share of EuroMTS. As expected, the EuroMTS information share is negatively related to the number of quote changes and positively related to the time-weighted proportion of locked and crossed quotes. In all, these results in combination with the graphical analysis of the economic significance in Figure 3.4 support our hypothesis H2 that the share of EuroMTS in the price discovery process of government bonds is larger for illiquid securities than for liquid bonds. The EuroMTS information share is larger for illiquid bonds than for liquid bonds. However, it can be seen from Tables 3.5 to 3.7 that the customer-dealer market remains the dominant market for almost all of the bonds in the sample. The results match the findings of the literature on the operational efficiency of open outcry and electronic trading mechanisms by Martens (1998).

Figure 3.4: Estimated Lower Bounds of the EuroMTS Information Shares Depending on the Number of Quote Changes in EuroMTS and the Proportion of Locked/Crossed Quotes

This figure plots the lower bound of the information shares of EuroMTS depending on the number of quote changes in EuroMTS and the proportion of locked/crossed quotes. The proportion of locked/crossed quotes is calculated on a time-weighted basis. The plot is based on the results of the cross section regression exhibited in the first column of Table VIII. All other explanatory variables are held constant at their sample mean.

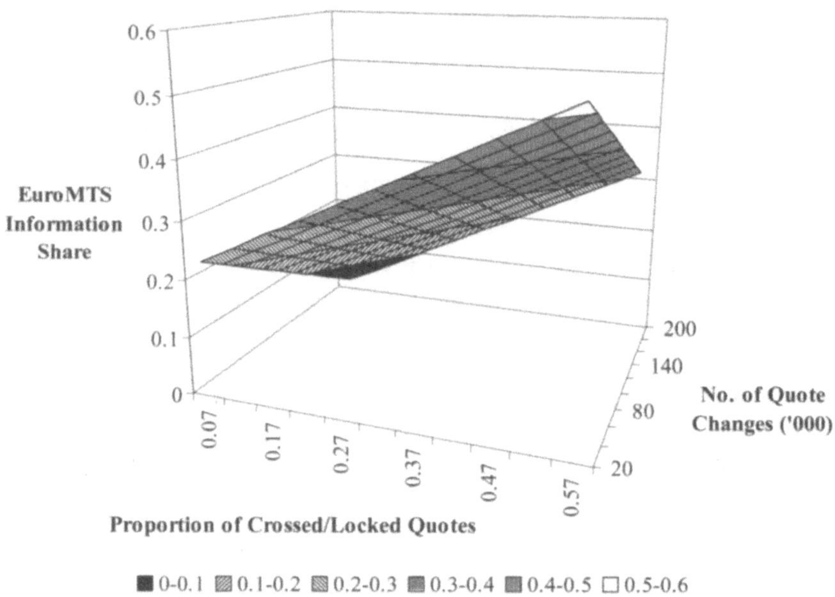

3.8 Conclusion

This article analyzes the short-run price dynamics between the interdealer market and the customer-dealer market for euro benchmark government bonds. All bonds in the sample are traded on the interdealer system EuroMTS during the observation period. Thereby, the focus lies on two questions. Which market contributes more to the price discovery? Is the share of the price contribution related to security characteristics? Hasbrouck's (1996, 2003) information share approach is applied to a unique integrated dataset containing quotes from EuroMTS as well as quotes for a representative sample of dealers from the customer-dealer market.

In contradiction to the commonly held belief that the interdealer market slightly leads the customer-dealer market,[115] we find that the EuroMTS share in the price discovery process for government bonds is dominated by the customer-dealer market. Additionally, we provide evidence that the information share of EuroMTS is larger for less liquid bonds than it is for liquid bonds. Especially the number of quote changes and the percentage of crossed and locked quotes have a significant impact on the interdealer market's information share. Nevertheless, we also find the customer-dealer market is the dominant market for almost all of the bonds in our sample.

The results are in line with the findings of Biais, Hillion and Spatt (1999), and Cao, Ghysels and Hatheway (2000), who both find indicative quotes do contain information. They are also in line with the results of Martens (1998) regarding the efficiency of electronic trading and open outcry systems. Continuous electronic trading systems contribute more to the price discovery process in periods with low volatility, while open outcry systems contribute more in periods of high volatility. In our case, liquid bonds trade more frequently. In this way, more information from trading is available for theses bonds. Conversely, the only information for illiquid bonds which are traded infrequently comes from the tradable quotes of EuroMTS.

The results also suggest, especially for very liquid bonds, the pricing error is smaller in the customer-dealer market. Although the customer-dealer sphere is more decentralized, collecting information from a sample of dealers from the customer-dealer market helps investors to avoid pricing errors. In turn, our findings indicate in the case of less liquid bonds, EuroMTS is the more dominant market. This supports the conclusion of Gravelle (2002). He emphasizes that the prevailing multiple-dealer structure in government bond markets is especially suited for illiquid securities, whereas the volume of an individual trade is still very large.[116] The fact that a dealer's customer order flow is not published in combination with the risk sharing opportunities in the interdealer market ensures that dealers are ready to trade even illiquid bonds with their customers.[117]

---

[115] For FX markets see, e.g., Lyons (2001), p. 115.

[116] See Section 4.8 in which the institutional trade sizes for corporate bonds and equities are compared, as well as Gravelle (2002), pp. 30-32.

[117] See Gravelle (2002), pp. 30-32.

This article provides further questions which are worth evaluating. As noted above, our sample contains only liquid bonds. Consequently, we cannot draw a final conclusion for the price discovery process of illiquid securities. Such relatively illiquid securities in government bond markets e.g. are emerging market bonds with a small outstanding amount and a low credit rating compared to the bonds in our sample. Trading in euro-denominated government securities of the ten new states which entered the European Union started in May 2004 on NewEuroMTS. As our results indicate, EuroMTS should be dominating the price discovery for these bonds.

Another question we cannot answer is whether individual dealers behave differently in the two market spheres in response to trades in the customer-dealer and the interdealer market respectively. The may help to answer the question whether dealer quotes reflect order flow information and are responsible for the observed price leadership.

4 Institutional Trading Costs in European Corporate Bond Markets

4.1 Introduction

In the past, researchers have extensively studied transaction costs in equity markets and found that implicit trading costs are economically significant. In contrast, few studies analyze transaction costs for institutional bond trades. Given the importance of worldwide bond markets, this seems surprising. The strong increase in the amount outstanding of euro-denominated bonds after the introduction of the euro exhibited in Figure 4.1 shows the growing importance of European corporate bond markets. But compared to the US, with an amount outstanding of $ 4.9 trillion,[118] the European market is still small. Even though the issuing activity was boosted by the introduction of the euro, the marketability and therefore liquidity of these issues is unexplored. In addition, the market for euro-denominated corporate bonds is still very opaque compared to the US market where the National Association of Securities Dealers (NASD) introduced its Trade Reporting and Compliance Engine (TRACE) on July 1, 2002 to publicly report OTC-transactions in corporate bonds. Edwards, Harris, and Piwowar (2004) and Bessembinder, Maxwell, and Venkataraman (2005) show that the dissemination of information on completed trades leads to a decrease in trading costs and thereby to an increase in liquidity.[119] The European market does not provide any post trade information to its investors and only the parties involved have knowledge on the existence of the trade.[120] As a whole, the European market is comparable to the US market before the introduction of TRACE in terms of transparency, but it is still less mature.

The differences between the European and the US corporate bond market motivate the first question addressed in this article: Does the lack of transparency and the smaller size of the European market translate into higher trading costs and are the determinants of the cost of trading the same? The second question we address is related to the field of asset allocation. Edwards, Harris and Piwowar (2004) analyze

---

118 The amount outstanding for the US market is an estimate by The Bond Market Association (2005b).

119 See Edwards, Harris, and Piwowar (2004), p. 26 and Bessembinder, Maxwell, and Venkataraman (2005), pp. 32-24.

120 An exception are trades on electronic multiple dealer systems in the customer-dealer market, some of which disseminate information on trade to the system's participants. See The Bond Market Association (2005a), p. 9.

institutional trades in investment grade corporate bonds in the US and infer that trading bonds is more expensive than trading stocks for small trade size.[121] This result is remarkable since the risk associated with bonds is usually much smaller than the risk of stocks. As a result, we analyze whether the costs of trading corporate bonds is more expensive than the costs of trading stocks. In order to provide a powerful explanation, we match the sample of institutional corporate bond trades with a sample of institutional trades in equities by the same issuers and directly compare the costs of trading in both asset classes.

Figure 4.1: Amount Outstanding of Bonds Issued by Euro Area Residents

This figure shows the amount outstanding of corporate bonds issued by non-monetary financial corporations and non-financial corporations which are residents of the euro area. The data on the amount outstanding is published in the Monthly Bulletin of the European Central Bank (ECB).

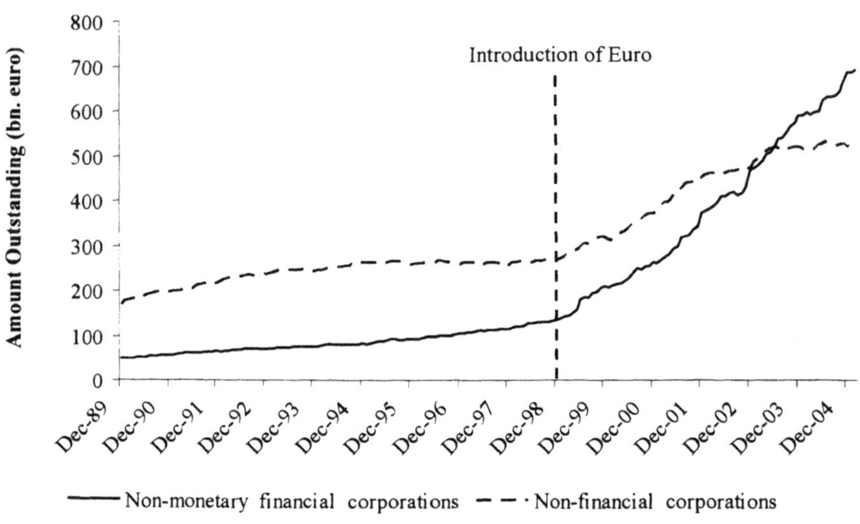

Apart from regulators, it is also important for several other parties to know the costs of trading corporate bonds. For investors, it is crucial to know the costs of trading bonds relative to the costs of trading equities. Significant cost differences might influence their capital allocation. The expected return of an asset class is one pivotal factor of the strategic and tactical asset allocation and has to be adjusted by the costs of

121 See Edwards, Harris, and Piwowar (2004), p. 16.

trading. If corporate bonds are more expensive to trade than equities, as found by Edwards, Harris and Piwowar (2004) for small trade sizes, their expected yield is relatively lower than under the assumption of equal costs for both asset classes. Therefore, an investor might attribute higher weights to equities relative to the case of equal costs.

It is important for investors to know the determinants of the costs as well. The decision to buy a certain bond depends on the expected yield over the investment horizon. If the liquidity of a bond varies with its characteristics, investors have to take this into account in the process of selecting the most favorable issue, to make sure that a possible advantage in the yield is not diluted by excess trading costs. If the costs of trading vary with the market conditions, investors who have no need for immediacy can afford to choose more favorable market conditions to conduct a trade, thus realizing lower average trading costs.

As noted by Edwards, Harris and Piwowar (2004), trading costs are also important for issuers.[122] Based on the findings of Amihud and Mendelson (1991), which show that bond liquidity influences yield to maturity and thus issuers cost of capital, they draw the conclusion that issuers should avoid bond characteristics which increase trading costs and decrease liquidity.[123] Accordingly, our results are of interest for companies planning to issue euro-denominated corporate bonds. Since we already know the costs of trading corporate bonds in the US market, our results might also have an impact on the decision of large issuers with access to both the US and the European markets when they chose the currency of their issue. Holding all other factors constant, differences in trading costs in these two markets result in different costs of capital for issues in euro and US dollars.

Our approach to measure the price impact of institutional costs as well as the data we use differs from the existing literature. The trades we analyze were directly collected by institutional investors and contain the exact time stamp of the transaction. Furthermore, we estimate the price impact by comparing transaction prices with current dealer quotes on a tick-by-tick basis. This approach allows us for the first time to

---

122 See Edwards, Harris and Piwowar (2004), p. 1.
123 See Amihud and Mendelson (1991), p. 1416.

directly determine the costs of trading corporate bonds and to identify past market conditions as an additional determinant of the trading costs.

Although it is plausible that the price impact of a trade should be related to current market conditions, only few transaction cost studies take this fact into account. Exceptions are Edwards and Wagner (1993) and Chiyachantana et al. (2004) with their analyses of the equity market, as well as Bessembinder, Maxwell, and Venkataraman (2005) for the US corporate bond market. While Edwards and Wagner (1993) show that timing costs vary strongly under the condition of large price movement, Chiyachantana et al. (2004) show that implicit trading costs are higher for liquidity demanding trades than for liquidity providing trades.[124] Bessembinder, Maxwell, and Venkataraman (2005) provide evidence that the trading activity in the five days prior to a trade has a negative impact on trading costs.[125] In extension to the existing literature, we use proxies for the momentum, the trading volume and the degree of dealer competition immediately before a transaction.

We analyze the price effect of corporate bond trades of 11 asset management firms from Germany, Austria, and the U.K. The companies have euro 840 billion assets under management (real estate investments excluded). According to the European Central Bank (2004), the assets of all euro area investment funds (mutual funds and institutional funds) were euro 2,248 billion by the end of the 3rd quarter 2003.

The data were collected from September 24, 2003 through December 19, 2003. Our sample contains 1,094 trades in euro corporate bonds with a total trading volume of euro 2.88 billion. The bond universe comprises 221 investment grade bonds with a total amount outstanding of euro 303.09 billion. To determine the trading costs, we match the trade data on quoted bid- and ask- prices of 23 different dealers and electronic customer-dealer platforms.

On average, we observe a significant price impact of 5.6 bp for institutional bond trades in our value-weighted sample. The costs are in line with the findings of Edwards, Harris, and Piwowar (2004) and Bessembinder, Maxwell, and Venkataraman

---

124 See Edwards and Wagner (1993), p. 68 and Chiyachantana et al (2004), pp. 883-885.

125 See Bessembinder, Maxwell, and Venkataraman (2005), p. 29.

(2005) for the US market after the introduction of TRACE.[126] Despite the opaqueness and the fact that the market is still young, European investment managers are able to trade at very low costs. The costs are very low compared to equity trading costs which are on average 69 bp in our sample. Using Plexus International Data, Chiyachantana et al. (2004) find implicit equity trading costs in developed countries between 3 bp and 63 bp for the period 1997-1998 and between 20 bp and 56 bp in 2001. To make the price impact of equities comparable with the price impact of corporate bonds, one has to add commission costs, which Chiyachantana et al. (2004) find to be between 9 bp and 57 bp for developed countries. Bikker, Spierdijk, and Sluis (2004) use data from the largest Dutch Pension fund and show that the average volume-weighted price impact is 19.6 bp for buys and 25.6 bp for sells. Based on the results from a survey among 27 German asset managers, Johanning and Schlenger (2002) estimate the costs of trading equities to be between 32 bp for passive funds and 62 bp for actively managed portfolios.[127]

Furthermore, we show that variables often found to be significantly related to the price impact of corporate bonds like the rating of the bond, the age of the issue, and the duration of the bond, do not influence the price impact of an institutional corporate bond trades in our sample. However, we do find evidence that the relative trade size, defined as the trade size divided by the amount outstanding, has a significant impact on trading costs. While some of the existing studies like Hong and Warga (2000), Schultz (2001), Chakravarty and Sarkar (2003), and Edwards, Harris and Piwowar (2004) find trading costs to decrease with trade size, we find a positive relation between relative trade size and trading costs.[128] We also provide important evidence that corporate bond trading costs are strongly influenced by the market conditions immediately before the trade. Price movements in the euro Bund futures, plus the trading volume in the Bund futures contract have a significant impact on trading costs. Finally, with an average

---

126 Edwards, Harris, and Piwowar (2004) find on average 7 bp one-way trading costs for a representative institutional trade size of $ 2 million and Bessembinder, Maxwell, and Venkataraman (2005) show that average one-way trading costs (for all trade sizes) are 6.7 bp for TRACE eligible bonds after the introduction of TRACE. See Edwards, Harris, and Piwowar (2004), p. 33 and Bessembinder, Maxwell, and Venkataraman (2005), p. 23.

127 See Johanning and Schlenger (2002), p. 94, Chiyachantana et al. (2004), p. 895, and Bikker, Spierdijk, and Sluis (2004), p. 9.

128 See Hong and Warga (2000), p. 39, Schultz (2001), pp. 692-693, and Edwards, Harris and Piwowar (2004), pp. 15-16. Hong and Warga (2000) find the negative relationship between effective spreads and dollar trade volume only for bonds traded on NYSE's Automated Bond System (ABS).

value-weighted price impact of 73.22 bp stocks of the same issuers are much more expensive to trade than corporate bonds.

The paper is organized as follows. Section 4.2 provides a review of the existing literature on bond trading costs. An overview on the organizational structure of institutional trading in euro corporate bonds is given in Section 4.3. Section 4.4 describes the data and provides some descriptive statistics. The methodology as well as the general results are explained in section 4.5. In section 4.6, possible determinants of the price impact are derived, and in section 4.7 we present the regression results and test the robustness of our results. In section 4.8 we compare the costs of trading highly liquid corporate bonds with the costs of trading highly liquid equities. Lastly, section 4.9 concludes.

4.2 Literature Review

While researchers have extensively studied equity trading costs, only little is known about the costs of trading corporate bonds. Early studies on the US market by Hong and Warga (2000), Schultz (2001), and Chakravarty and Sarkar (2003) analyze transaction costs based on a sample of trades executed on behalf of insurance companies provided by Capital Access International (CAI) before the introduction of TRACE. Hong and Warga (2000) as well as Chakravarty and Sarkar (2003) calculate the effective spread for each bond as the average of daily realized spreads by taking the dollar-volume-weighted average price executed at the ask-price each day and subtracting the like figure for transactions at the bid-price. Hong and Warga (2000) find round trip costs of 13.28 bp for investment grade bonds (Aaa-Baa) including treasuries and agencies and 19.13 bp for non-investment grade bonds.[129] Chakravarty and Sarkar (2003) find a mean effective spread for corporate bonds of 21 cents per $ 100 par value for their full sample and 28 cents per $ 100 par value using only non-investment grade bonds.[130] To avoid the requirement of at least one buy and one sell per day, Schultz (2001) employs a methodology that differs from the above-cited studies. He uses bid quotes on a month end basis and approximates for the intra-month price change in a corporate bond using the change in the price of a treasury bond with similar duration. Then he regresses the

[129] See Hong and Warga (2000), p. 36.
[130] See Chakravarty and Sarkar (2003), p. 41.

difference between the trade price and the estimated bid price on a dummy variable that takes a value of one for buys and zero for sells to determine round-trip trading costs. For investment grade bonds Schultz (2001) reports round-trip costs of 27 cents per $ 100 par value.[131] In contrast to these studies, we use trades in euro-denominated corporate bonds conducted by investment management firms. The investment managers provided a time stamp down to the minute for each trade. Together with the bid- and ask-quotes on a tick-by-tick basis, we are able to calculate the price impact of each trade without relying on the effective spread as a measure of trading costs or estimating the midquote on a daily basis.

The more recent studies of Edwards, Harris, and Piwowar (2004) and Bessembinder, Maxwell, and Venkataraman (2005) both estimate indicator variable regression models with different explanatory variables in their analyses. Both studies analyze the impact of the introduction of TRACE on the costs of trading corporate bonds. Edwards, Harris and Piwowar (2004) employ the methodology of Harris and Piwowar (2004) to the TRACE (Trade Reporting and Compliance Engine) dataset from the NASD (National Association of Securities Dealers).[132] Their data contains all OTC trades in all corporate bonds for the year 2003, including those not made public through TRACE. They show that effective half spreads in corporate bonds average 69 bp for a representative trade size of $ 20,000. For institutional trade sizes, effective spreads are much lower. The effective half spread for a trade size of $ 2 million is 7 bp. Trading costs are lower for bonds whose trades are published through TRACE.[133] Arguing that the round-trip costs for retail sized trades in equity markets average less than 40 bp, they find the costs of trading corporate bonds especially for retail sized trades more expensive than the costs of trading equities.[134] Bessembinder, Maxwell, and Venkataraman (2005) rely on the corporate bond transactions provided by CAI. They measure execution costs of institutional corporate bond trades before and after the initiation of public transaction reporting for some bonds through TRACE in July 2002. Using an indicator model that allows for the effect of observable public information on the underlying bond value, they estimate a half-spread of 13.4 bp for TRACE-eligible

131 See Schultz (2001), p. 686. For a detailed description of the methodology, see also Schultz (2001), pp. 680-684.

132 See Harris and Piwowar (2004), pp. 15-22 as well as Edwards, Harris, and Piwowar (2004), pp. 10-14.

133 See Edwards, Harris, and Piwowar (2004), p. 15 and 33.

134 See Edwards, Harris, and Piwowar (2004), p. 16 and 23 as well as pp. 38-39. For the methodology see also pp. 10-14.

corporate bonds and 20.14 bp for non-TRACE-eligible corporate bonds during the 6 months prior to the initiation of public reporting. For the 6 months after the initiation, execution costs decrease to 6.7 bp for TRACE-eligible bonds and 16.26 bp for non-TRACE-eligible bonds.[135]

Even though Bessembinder, Maxwell, and Venkataraman (2005) use only institutional trades in their sample, our analysis differs from both studies in several respects. We analyze trading costs for the European corporate bond market which is much less transparent and developed than the US market after the introduction of TRACE. In contrast to both studies, we calculate the price impact directly from trade prices and current market quotes and do not rely on econometric models for the determination of the "fair price" of a bond.

4.3 The Market for Corporate Bonds

Bond markets are over-the-counter multiple-dealer markets. In contrast to multiple-dealership equity markets (such as NASDAQ), corporate bond markets are decentralized.[136] As a consequence, the amount of information available to the public on a consolidated basis is very small. In multiple-dealership equity markets, pre-trade information (quotes across dealers) plus post-trade information (completed trades) is available on one Bloomberg or Reuters screen. As in equity markets, dealer quotes for bonds are published via information systems, but most of these quotes are indicative and the volume a dealer is ready to trade at the quoted price is not published. To get the best tradeable price, an investor has to contact each single dealer to actively explore the best quotation in the market. In other words, in decentralized markets, simultaneous transactions with identical order characteristics can occur at different prices and, more importantly, at prices other than the best available price. Another distinguishing feature of bond markets is the existence of two different trading environments: a public environment where customers (buy side investors) trade with liquidity providers, and an interdealer environment where liquidity providers trade with each other. Since we are interested in the trading costs of institutional buy side investors, we analyze exclusively trades between customers and dealers in the public trading environment.

135 See Bessembinder, Maxwell, and Venkataraman (2005), p. 23

136 For an overview on dealership markets see Gravelle (2002).

Although the organization of institutional trading is very similar, there are also differences between the US and the European corporate bond market. The US bond market is gradually becoming more transparent. In an effort to bring greater transparency, the National Association of Securities Dealers (NASD) began to publicly report transactions in corporate bonds through its Trade Reporting and Compliance Engine (TRACE) on July 1, 2002. This rule first applied to 498 issues with issuance size of at least $ 1 billion. While the NASD required the reporting of the transaction within 1 hour and 15 minutes of the time of execution in 2001, transactions have to be reported within 15 minutes from July 1, 2005. In contrast, European bond markets are rather opaque. Completed trades are usually reported only to the parties involved, so that investors cannot compare their trade price with the trade prices of other market participants.[137]

4.4 Data and Descriptive Statistics

The data used in this study were provided by the German investment consultant alpha portfolio advisors GmbH and were used for their consulting services. Each manager's trading costs were compared to the trading costs of the peer group. Eleven asset management firms based in Austria, Germany, and the U.K. collected trades for 62 trading days from September 25, 2003 through December 19, 2003. Even though most of the asset managers offer their customers to manage their portfolios actively as well as passively, more than 98% of the portfolios in our study are actively managed.[138] The companies had altogether euro 841.8 billion assets under management by the end of September 2003. The smallest manager had less than euro 10 billion, while the largest manager had more than euro 250 billion assets under management. Table 4.1 compares the assets under management of our sample of asset management firms with the European investment industry. The 11 managers reported euro 841 billion assets under management. As reported by the European Central Bank (ECB), the assets under

137 At least in some countries, transactions in exchange listed bonds have to be reported and are disseminated by the exchange on the same day or the following day. Details can be found in International Organization of Securities Commissions (2004).

138 The proportion of actively managed portfolios is based on the data of 8 asset managers who reported the style of their funds.

management of all euro area funds were euro 3,085.6 billion.[139] Therefore, our sample covers approximately 27 % of European investment management industry. Considering only bonds, the 11 asset managers reported having euro 394.8 billion invested in bonds. That equals approximately 24 % of the assets under management of all euro area funds, invested in bond and mixed funds less mixed funds' holdings in shares and other equity.

Table 4.1: Assets under Management of the 11 Asset Managers

This table provides an overview on the assets under management of the 11 participating asset managers. The data on total assets under management for our sample and on assets under management invested in bonds, European bonds, and corporate bonds are based on self-reported data. The assets under management of fund managers in the euro area are based on the monthly bulletin of the European Central Bank (2004).

Assets under Management (September 30, 2003)	Sample	Population
Total Assets under Management	841.8	3,085.6
Assets under Management Invested in Bonds	394.8	1,406.7

Table 4.2 gives a survey on the analyzed bond universe. It comprises the 197 largest bonds of the iBoxx EUR Corporates index plus 24 additional bonds considered important for the study by the participants. The bonds analyzed have at least 1.5 years to maturity, euro 0.7 billon issuing volume and have an investment grade rating.[140] Out of the 221 corporate bonds, 14 are rated AAA, 44 are rated AA, 100 are rated A, and 63 bonds are rated BBB. The amount outstanding of the sample is euro 303.09 billion – euro 19.50 billion in AAA rated bonds, euro 56.99 billion in AA rated bonds, euro 132.05 billion in A rated bonds, and euro 94.55 billion in BBB rated bonds. The relative amount outstanding and the relative number of bonds within different rating categories is almost the same. The sample has an average time to maturity (weighted by amount outstanding) of 6.8 years, and an average weighted age of 2.31 years. The average weighted duration is 4.91.

139 See European Central Bank (2004), p. 2425 of the euro area statistics money, banking and investment funds.

140 To be included in the iBoxx € Corporates index, a bond needs to have a minimum time to maturity of 1 year and an amount outstanding of at least euro 500 million. The index also comprises bonds by non-euro area residents that issued euro-denominated bonds.

Each asset manager collected the trades for a representative sample of funds. In all, the sample comprises 1,018 different funds.[141] The participants of the study reported the date and time of the transaction, the transaction price, the trade size, and the ISIN of the bond. Each trade has a dummy variable indicating if the transaction was a sale or a purchase. To complete our dataset we added information on bond and issuer characteristics like duration, time to maturity, time since issuance, amount outstanding, rating, information on whether the bond is callable, and the market capitalization if the issuer is exchange listed.

Table 4.2: Descriptive Statistics of the Analyzed Bond Universe

This table provides an overview on the bonds that qualified for the transaction cost study. The average maturity, the average duration and the average age are weighted by the amount outstanding.

Bond Universe		
Number of Bonds	221	*100.00%*
Rating AAA	14	*6.33%*
Rating AA	44	*19.91%*
Rating A	100	*45.25%*
Rating BBB	63	*28.51%*
Amount Outstanding Sample (bn. euro)	303.09	*100.00%*
Rating AAA	19.50	*6.43%*
Rating AA	56.99	*18.80%*
Rating A	132.05	*43.57%*
Rating BBB	94.55	*31.20%*
Average maturity (in years)	6.80	
Average duration	4.91	
Average age (in years)	2.31	

141 If a bond was traded for at least one fund in the sample and e.g. one fund not covered by the sample, the pooled order size was reported.

The 11 asset managers reported a total of 2,672 trades. Trades reported by the same asset manager for different funds in the same bond and at the same time are treated as one pooled transaction. This pooling reduces the number of observations to 1,187. Missing quotes lead to another reduction of the sample size to 1,094 trades.

Table 4.3 exhibits the descriptive statistics of these institutional trades. Out of the 221 corporate bonds in the universe, the participating asset managers traded only 182 different bonds during the observation period. These 182 bonds have a joint amount outstanding of euro 258.14 billion. The average trade size in our sample is euro 2.63 million. This leads to an overall market value of euro 2.88 billion for the 1,094 trades. The average traded nominal value is euro 2.48 million and the total traded nominal value is euro 2.72 billion respectively. The average time to maturity weighted by nominal trade size in our sample of institutional bond trades is 8.05 years, which is about one year longer than the weighted average of the bond universe with 6.8 years. The average weighted duration with 5.59 is also higher than in the bond universe, while the average weighted age of the traded bonds is about 0.4 lower than in the universe. The data contains 539 buy- and 555 sell-transactions. The average trade size is smaller for buys than for sells. This is consistent with the empirical evidence for institutional equity trades.[142] The average weighted maturity and the average weighted duration are also larger for buys than for sells. The average age is almost the same.

The institutional trade data is matched on a dataset of indicative quotes from 23 different dealers. For the analyzed 62-day period, 124 million quotes on a tick-by-tick basis were collected from Bloomberg L.P. After aggregating the data on a minute-by-minute basis, we filter the quote data to eliminate obvious errors that might bias the price impact. Within the same one-minute-interval, we delete the bid and ask quote of a dealer if the bid- (ask-) quote is larger (smaller) than the ask- (bid-) quote of every other dealer. If we observe this pattern in an interval with quotes by only two dealers, we delete both dealers' quotes. Afterwards, we delete price changes (with reversal) of more than 1.5% on a one-minute basis. However, a comparison of the results before and after the filtering shows that the magnitude and the significance of the price impact remains

[142] See, among others, Chiyachantana et al. (2004), pp. 876-877, Chan and Lakonishok (1993), p. 181, and Keim, and Madhavan (1997), pp. 270-271. Using Plexus data Chiyachantana et al. (2004) find an average dollar volume per trading decision of $1.19 million. The average dollar value in the sample of institutional trades in Chan and Lakonishok (1993) is $304,000 for buys and $335,000 for sells. Keim and Madhavan (1997) observe median institutional trade sizes of $138,100 for buys and $385,900 for sells.

the same. Furthermore, since we cannot observe when a quote is cancelled or becomes invalid, we delete each quote after five minutes to make sure that the estimate of the trading costs is not biased due to obsolete quotes.[143]

Table 4.3: Descriptive Statistics of the Institutional Trade Data

In this table, we provide descriptive information on the observed corporate bond trades for the whole sample as well as for buys and sells separately. The average maturity, the average duration and the average age are weighted with the nominal value of the trades.

Trade and Quote Data	All Trades	Buys	Sells
Number of Trades	1,094	539	555
% of trades	*100.00%*	*49.27%*	*50.73%*
Number of Trades by Rating			
AAA	28	7	21
*% of trades**	*2.56%*	*1.30%*	*3.78%*
AA	115	54	61
*% of trades**	*10.51%*	*10.02%*	*10.99%*
A	512	236	276
*% of trades**	*46.80%*	*43.78%*	*49.73%*
BBB	439	242	197
*% of trades**	*40.13%*	*44.90%*	*35.50%*
Amount Outstanding Traded Bonds (bn. euro)	258.14	221.14	224.67
Number of Different Bonds Traded	182	152	157
Trades per Day	17.65	8.69	8.95
Avg. trade size (m. €)	2.63	2.27	2.97
Avg. traded nominal value (m. €)	2.48	2.13	2.83
Avg. maturity traded	8.05	9.39	7.07
Avg. duration traded	5.59	6.08	5.23
Avg. age traded	1.90	1.91	1.89

* % of trades in column

143 The time period of five minutes is plausible for 2 reasons: i) we usually observe a time series based on one minute intervals without gaps for dealers that are active in a certain bond. ii) Especially in times when scheduled macroeconomic information arrives at the market, prices can move really fast. This kind of information is distributed at a fixed time of day and every market participant gets this information at the same time. If the dealer doesn't want to distribute new quotes to the other market participants because he is not sure about the implication of the information, an old quote of the dealer can already deviate from the actual market price very strongly.

Since we observe crossed or locked quotes in 16% of the one-minute intervals in our sample period, we lose many observations if we use the best bid- and ask- quotes to calculate the midprice. Therefore, we decided to calculate the midprice in three different ways. Firstly, we use the average bid- and average ask- price per one-minute interval. Secondly, we eliminate the lowest bid- and the highest ask-quote from our sample. In case we observe only one bid- and one ask-quote, we keep this observation unchanged. Thirdly, to validate our results, we use the inside spread and calculate the price impact for a sub-sample of trades.

Figure 4.2: Quoted Inside Spread by the Time of Day and Rating

This figure exhibits the average inside spread by the time of day and bond rating. The inside spread was calculated for each one-minute interval and then averaged across time and bonds in the same rating category.

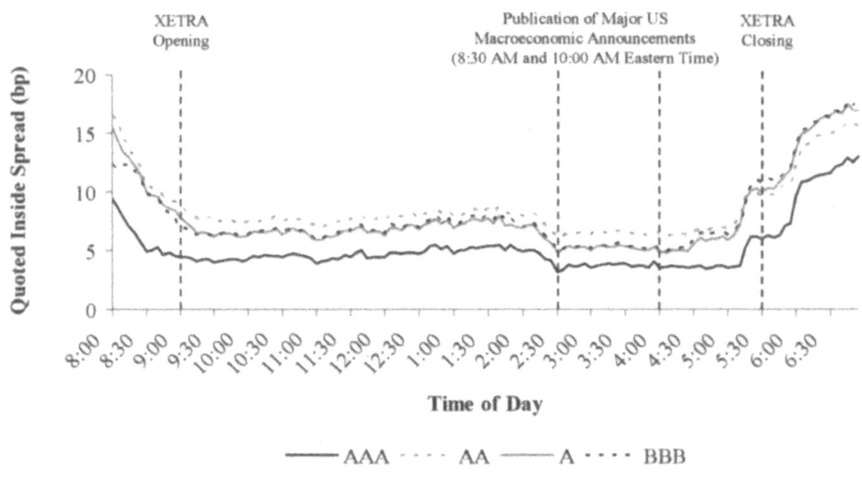

The inside spread in Figure 4.2 exhibits the typical U-shaped pattern.[144] It is smaller for AAA-rated bonds than for the lower rated bonds. The difference is one to two bp in the afternoon and up to 10 bp in the evening. Until 5:30 pm, we find the inside spread of AA-rated bonds to be slightly higher than the inside spread of A-and BBB-rated bonds. For an A-rated bond, we observe an inside spread of about 14 bp in

---

[144] Because we do not observe any institutional trades before 8:30 a.m. and after 7:00 pm, we only take quotes between 8:00 a.m. and 7:00 pm into account for the descriptive analysis of the indicative quotes.

the morning that drops to 5 bp in the afternoon and increases to 17 bp in the evening again.

4.5 Methodology and General Results

4.5.1 Methodology – Measuring the Price Impact

We define the price impact as the difference between the trade price and the unperturbed price in basis points.[145] The unperturbed price is the price that would prevail if the trade had not occurred. The midquote is a proxy for the fair market value of a bond at the time of the transaction. To determine a bond's midquote, we first calculate its mean bid-quote and mean ask-quote for each trading minute. These quotes represent the average reservation price of all observed dealers to sell or buy a specific bond. The prevailing midquote of a bond at time *t* is calculated as half of the sum of the mean bid- and ask-quote

$$(4.1) \qquad Midquote_t = \frac{\frac{1}{B}\sum_{n=1}^{B} P_{t,n}^{b} + \frac{1}{A}\sum_{n=1}^{A} P_{t,n}^{a}}{2},$$

where *A* (*B*) is the prevailing number of asks (bids) in the interval, and $P_{t,n}^{a}$ ($P_{t,n}^{b}$) is the ask- (bid-) price of dealer *n* in interval *t*. Due to the high proportion of negative inside spreads we observe in the quote data, we use average bid- and ask-prices to calculate the midprice. The pre-execution benchmark is calculated with on average 8.4 bid- and the like figure of ask-quotes. To test the robustness of our results, we also conduct our analysis using the best bid- and the best ask-price, as well as using the average bid- (ask-) price but excluding the lowest (highest) quoted price, to calculate the midprice.

The price impact *PI* of bond *i* at time *t* is then calculated as

$$(4.2) \qquad PI_{i,t} = \frac{(P_{i,t} - Midquote_{i,t-1})}{Midquote_{i,t-1}} \times S,$$

[145] The time of the trading decision and the time of the transaction need not to be the same since internal order approval can lead to a delay. Unfortunately, we cannot observe the exact time of the trading decision. Opportunity costs such as waiting or timing costs are therefore neglected in our analysis.

where $P_{i,t}$ is the execution price of bond i at time t, and S is a binary variable that takes a value of one for buys and minus one for sells. We take only those institutional trades into account where we observe a bid- and ask-quote in the five minutes before the trade.

4.5.2 General Results

The difference in the results from the equal-weighted and the value-weighted samples in the existing literature on equity markets indicate the importance of the dollar value of a trade. As a consequence, we focus in our study on the value-weighted results. Table 4.4 shows the general results using the methodology outlined above. The first three columns exhibit the price impact for the midquote calculated with average bid- and ask-prices. On a value-weighted basis, we find an average price impact of 5.60 bp. The price impact of purchases with 5.12 bp is only slightly lower than the price impact of sells with 5.96 bp. We calculate the midquote used in the next three columns by eliminating the lowest bid- (highest ask-) quote from the calculation of the average bid- (ask-) quote. The price impact differs only slightly from the first three columns. It is about 0.2 bp lower for buys and 0.22 bp lower for sells, resulting in a total value-weighted price impact of 5.39 bp. The last three columns show the average value-weighted price impact for the sub-sample, using the best bid- and the best ask-quote to calculate the midquote. The price impact for buys is higher than in the sample using average quoted bid- and ask-prices to calculate the midquote, while the price impact for sells is lower. The total price impact decreases slightly by 0.04 bp. Performing a t-test on the difference of the costs of buying and selling corporate bonds does not reject the hypothesis that the difference equals zero on a 10% significance level. Hence, we continue reporting only average costs in the remaining tables. For all three methodologies, we find the costs of trading corporate bonds increase with trade size. Depending on methodology, the price impact for the smallest trade size category is between 2.0 bp and 2.65 bp, the price impact for the largest trade size category is between 8 bp and 8.8 bp. This result contradicts Schultz (2001) and Edwards, Harris and Piwowar (2004).[146] They find the trade size to be negatively related to the trading costs.

---

[146] See Schultz (2001), pp. 692-693, and Edwards, Harris and Piwowar (2004), pp. 15-16.

Overall, the price impact of trades in euro-denominated corporate bonds is surprisingly small. It is in line with the existing literature for the US corporate bond markets after the introduction of TRACE, but they are lower than the round trip costs of 27 cents per $ 100 par value before the introduction of TRACE, reported by Schultz (2001).[147]

4.6 Possible Determinants of the Price Impact

In our analysis we consider three groups of determinants that may influence effective spreads in European bond markets: trade and bond characteristics, market conditions, and money manager specific determinants. In this section, we explain the variables of the three groups and provide arguments for a potential influence.

4.6.1 Trade, Bond, and Issuer Characteristics

There is empirical and theoretical evidence that trade characteristics as well as bond characteristics have an influence on trading costs. While age and amount outstanding are measures of the tradeability, duration and bond rating capture the effects of price sensitivity to interest rate changes and default risk on transaction cost. Some studies also show that an attached option influences the trading costs of a bond as well.

---

[147] See Schultz (2001), p. 686.

Table 4.4: Price Impact of Trading Corporate Bonds

This table exhibits the volume-weighted average price impact for all trades in European corporate bonds, as well as the volume-weighted average price impact for buys and sells separately. The results are based on different benchmarks. The first three columns present the price impact of trading European corporate bonds based on the midquote that is determined using the average bid- and the average ask-price. For the results in the next three columns, the midquote is calculated using the average bid- and ask-price after excluding the lowest bid- and the highest ask-price. If we only observed one bid or one ask quote in an interval, this quote was retained. In the last three columns, the midprice used to calculate the price impact is based on the best- bid and the best ask-price. This reduces our sample since we do not use midquotes for the calculation of the price impact that are older than five minutes. This restriction is used to avoid the use obsolete quotes in times when prices change quickly.

	Midquote based on average bid/ask			**Midquote based on average bid/ask w/o lowest bid and highest ask**			**Midquote based on best bid/ask**		
	All trades	Buys	Sells	All trades	Buys	Sells	All trades	Buys	Sells
Mean	5.6042	5.1246	5.9602	5.3882	4.9206	5.7354	5.5651	5.8849	5.3288
std	*0.3920*	*0.5855*	*0.5298*	*0.3888*	*0.5794*	*0.5265*	*0.4479*	*0.7010*	*0.5790*
Median	3.9968	2.8968	4.8501	4.2091	2.6153	4.5319	4.2200	3.7351	4.4203
< euro 0.5M	1.9553	2.3839	1.3149	2.0173	2.6071	1.1361	2.645	3.3461	1.5965
euro 0.5-5M	3.4260	3.3918	3.4524	3.3654	3.5296	3.2393	2.715	3.8699	1.7705
euro 5-10M	5.1778	5.3381	5.0707	4.7505	4.9151	4.6405	5.2884	6.1363	4.7511
> euro 10M	8.2264	6.9647	9.1433	7.9947	6.5326	9.0572	8.8111	8.1732	9.2599
N	1,094	539	555	1,094	539	555	880	438	442

Duration: Like the time to maturity, the duration captures the bond's exposure to interest-rate-changes. Therefore, we expect the variable to be positively related to trading costs. Evidence for this relationship in corporate bond markets is provided by Hong and Warga (2000), Schultz (2001), Chakravarty and Sarkar (2003), and Edwards, Harris and Piwowar (2004).[148] We do not include the time to maturity in our model since it is strongly correlated to the duration.

Age: Sarig and Warga (1989), Amihud and Mendelson (1991), as well as Alexander, Edwards, and Ferri (2000) suggest that the age of a bond, measured as its time since issuance, should be related to liquidity. They expect that, with increasing age of a bond, the fraction of the bond's issue absorbed into institutional investors portfolios increases and, consequently, its liquidity decreases.[149] Hong and Warga (2000), Chakravarty and Sarkar (2003), and Edwards, Harris, and Piwowar (2004) confirm this result for the corporate bond market.[150]

Rating: Merton (1974) and Leland (1994) for example suggest that the bond price should also depend on the probability of default.[151] Edwards, Harris, and Piwowar (2004), and Chakravarty and Sarkar (2003) support the hypothesis of increasing spread with increasing credit risk.[152]

Callable: Since an attached put increases the complexity of the bond, we would expect higher transaction costs for callable bonds. On the other hand, Edwards, Harris, and Piwowar (2004) provide evidence that bonds with attached puts are cheaper to trade.[153]

Trade Size and Amount Outstanding: In contrast to the findings in equity markets, Schultz (2001) and Edwards, Harris and Piwowar (2004) provide empirical

---

148 See Hong and Warga (2000), pp. 38-39, Schultz (2001), p. 698, Chakravarty and Sarkar (2003) p. 44, and Edwards, Harris and Piwowar (2004), p. 20.

149 See Sarig and Warga (1989), p. 369, Amihud and Mendelson (1991), p. 1413, and Alexander, Edwards, and Ferri (2000), pp. 178-179 and p. 200.

150 See Hong and Warga (2000), pp. 38-39,Chakravarty and Sarkar (2003), p. 44, and Edwards, Harris, and Piwowar (2004), p. 20.

151 See Merton (1974), p. 449 and Leland (1994), p. 1213.

152 See Edwards, Harris, and Piwowar (2004), p. 23 and Chakravarty and Sarkar (2003), p. 44.

153 See Edwards, Harris, and Piwowar (2004), p. 21.

evidence that trading costs decrease with trade size in corporate bond markets, indicating, that a fixed cost component is important to bond market transactions.[154]

Another liquidity variable possibly with an impact on the costs of trading corporate bonds is the amount outstanding. Garbade and Silber (1976) show that the amount outstanding is negatively related to a dealer's quoted bid-ask spread. A larger amount outstanding results in a larger quantity potentially available for trade and therefore higher marketability.[155] Hong and Warga (2000), Edwards, Harris, and Piwowar (2004), and Schultz (2001) confirm this hypothesis for the corporate bond market.[156]

Seen as a whole, a traded face value of euro 10 million in a bond with an amount outstanding of euro 1 billion is relatively more than a traded face value of euro 30 million in the same bond. As a consequence of this, we decided to include the relative trade size, measured as the traded face value as a fraction of the amount outstanding in our analysis.

Market Capitalization of the Issuer: From equity markets, we know that firm size has a negative impact on trading costs.[157] The deduction is reasonable that the same relation holds for bonds since more information is revealed on larger issuers because of better analyst coverage and presence in media.

4.6.2 Market Conditions

As far as we know, the impact of the market conditions on transaction costs in corporate bond markets has rarely been studied in the empirical literature.[158] One reason is the

---

154 See Schultz (2001), p. 692 and p.696 as well as Edwards, Harris and Piwowar (2004), pp. 15-16.

155 See, among others, Garbade and Silber (1976), p. 739.

156 See Hong and Warga (2000), pp. 38-39, Schultz (2001), pp. 692-693 and p. 696, and Edwards, Harris, and Piwowar (2004), p. 18 and p. 21. In Hong and Warga (2000), the amount outstanding has only a significant impact on the costs on ABS trades but not on the costs of trades in the CAI data.

157 See, e.g., Keim and Madhavan (1998), p. 58 and Chan and Lakonishok (1997), p. 724.

158 Exceptions are Hong and Warga (2000) and Bessembinder, Maxwell, and Venkataraman (2005). Hong and Warga (2000) use the squared bond return in the month of the transaction to take bond-specific information (as measured by bond-specific volatility) into account. Both studies focus on measures over a longer time horizon than ours do and are therefore less suited for market timing purposes. Their empirical analysis shows that transaction costs increase with squared return and, therefore, with increasing uncertainty. Bessembinder, Maxwell, and Venkataraman (2005) provide evidence, that the trading activity in the five days prior to a trade has a negative impact on trading costs.

poor availability of trade- and quote-data in bond markets. But even for equity markets where post- as well as pre-trade information is available, only few studies focus on market conditions. Our data contains exact time stamps on a minute-by-minute basis reported by the participating investment managers. Together with the quote data from Bloomberg, we have a powerful dataset which allows us to examine the impact of actual market conditions on the transaction costs in bond markets.

Momentum: In their study for the equity market, Edwards and Wagner (1993) find the most important factor affecting timing costs is whether a trade supplies liquidity to the market or demands liquidity. A sale at decreasing prices demands liquidity and should therefore be more expensive than a purchase. Chiyachantana et al. (2004) also provide evidence that trading with the trend of the market is more expensive than providing liquidity to the market.[159]

Since Schultz (2001) provides evidence, that two thirds of the price change of a corporate bond can be explained by the price change of a government bond with similar characteristics, we include the return of the Bund futures contract with the shortest maturity in our model.[160] The Bund futures price change is an adequate measure for expectation changes about future inflation and the momentum of the market.

Trading Volume:[161] Chakravarty and Sarkar (2003) find smaller effective spreads on days with high trading volume, while Hong and Warga (2000) do not find a significant impact of the daily trading volume on the effective spread of corporate bonds. Bessembinder, Maxwell, and Venkataraman (2005) provide evidence, that the trading activity in the five days prior to a trade has a negative impact on trading costs.[162] For equities on the other hand, Foster and Viswanathan (1993) find empirical evidence that trading volume and trading costs are higher in the first half hour of trading at the

---

159 See Edwards and Wagner (1993), p. 68 and Chiyachantana et al (2004), pp. 883-885.

160 See Schultz (2001), pp. 682-683.

161 We also used the volatility before the trade as an explanatory variable. The volatility and the trading volume turned out to be strongly correlated. Since the use of the trading volume leads to better results, we decided to exclude the volatility from our analysis. For equity markets, Foster and Viswanathan (1993) confirm the positive intraday relationship between trading volume and return volatility. See Foster and Viswanathan (1993), p. 201.

162 See Chakravarty and Sarkar (2003), p. 44, Hong and Warga (2000), pp. 38-39, and Bessembinder, Maxwell, and Venkataraman (2005), pp. 28-29. Although Hong and Warga (2000) do not find daily trade volume to be related with institutional corporate bond trades, they find a significant negative relationship for ABS trades with much smaller average trade size.

New York Stock Exchange.[163] Due to the low degree of centralization of the European corporate bond markets, trades are not observable and hence not recorded. To incorporate effects of the trading volume on transaction costs, we include the trading volume in the EUREX Bund futures contract with the shortest maturity[164] as a proxy for trading activity in our model.

Competition: The competition for customer order flow among dealers is another variable that reflects actual market conditions. Tinic and West (1973) and Benston and Hagerman (1974) for example show, that the costs of dealer services decrease with the number of dealers and thus with increasing competition.[165] If more active dealers are observed in an electronic information system like Bloomberg, this could be a signal for higher competition for customer order flow. To capture the effects of competition in our model, we incorporate the number of active dealers as explanatory variable.[166]

4.6.3 Money Manager Specific Determinants

Chan and Lakonishok (1995) examine the behavior of stock prices around institutional trades. In their analysis, dummy variables for the identity of the money managers contribute significantly to the overall explanatory power of the econometric model.[167]

Keim and Madhavan (1997) analyze the variation in equity trading costs across individual institutions. They can reject the hypothesis that the base-level transaction costs are equal even within investment styles. Keim and Madhavan (1997) conclude that the differences in trading costs reflect differences in the skills and abilities of different institutions.[168]

---

163 See Foster and Viswanathan (1993), pp. 209-210.

164 The contract with the shortest maturity is the most actively traded contract during our observation period. Therefore one can assume most investors process their changes in interest rate expectations in this contract.

165 See Tinic and West (1973), p. 1721 and Benston and Hagerman (1974), p. 355 and p. 360. A discussion of several types of competition can be found in Demsetz (1968), pp. 43-45.

166 Dealers providing updated quotes within the 5-minute interval before the transaction are defined as active dealers.

167 See Chan and Lakonishok (1995), pp. 1164-1165.

168 See Keim and Madhavan (1997), pp. 288-290.

For the US corporate bond market, Schultz (2001) shows that trading costs are lower for active institutions than for inactive institutions.[169]

Since we know the identity of the asset managers, we build three different size categories based on the assets under management to capture possible size-related effects on trading costs. Size could have an impact on trading costs because dealers have an incentive to provide better prices for larger institutions for two reasons. Firstly, a larger investor is a more important customer for the dealer in terms of trading volume, and secondly, the order flow of large institutions might convey more information.

4.7 Determinants of the Price Impact for Corporate Bonds - Regression Results and Robustness Checks

4.7.1 Regression Results

We estimate several regression models to determine the factors that influence the price impact of corporate bonds. The model is based on intraday return and volume data since we expect that the market conditions prior to the trade have a large effect on trading costs. More specifically, we use return and volume data for the last 30 minutes before the trade was conducted. This time period seems to be sufficient, considering the quick processing of macroeconomic information in bond markets.[170]

The full model for the regression analysis using intraday data is specified as:

$$
\begin{aligned}
PI_i = {} & \beta_0 + \beta_1 \cdot Callable + \beta_2 \cdot Duration + \beta_3 \cdot Age + \beta_4 \cdot Relative\,Trade\,Size \\
& + \beta_5 \cdot Rating\,AA + \beta_6 \cdot Rating\,A + \beta_7 \cdot Rating\,BBB \\
& + \beta_8 \cdot Market\,Capitalization + \beta_9 \cdot Active\,Dealers \\
& + \beta_{10} \cdot Volume\,Bund\,Future + \beta_{11} \cdot Momentum\,Bund\,Future \\
& + \beta_{12} \cdot Medium\,Manager + \beta_{13} \cdot Large\,Manager \\
& + \beta_{14} \cdot Momentum\,Bund\,Future * Volume\,Bund\,Future + \varepsilon_i\,.
\end{aligned}
\tag{4.3}
$$

[169] See Schultz (2001), p. 695.

[170] E.g. Fleming and Remolona (1999) show that macroeconomic announcements induce nearly instantaneous changes in the market conditions and Hautsch and Hess (2002) show that the volatility of the T-bond futures decreases to its base volatility within about 30 minutes after the announcement of macroeconomic information. See Fleming and Remolona (1999), pp. 1906-1908 and Hautsch and Hess (2002), p. 157.

An explanation of the independent variables can be found in Table 4.5. All return variables are calculated for the last 30 minutes before the minute of the trade. White's (1980) heteroscedasticity-consistent covariance matrix is used to calculate the standard errors.

Table 4.5: Explanation of the independent variables in the regression models

In this table, we provide information on the explanatory variables used in the regression model.

Variable	
Callable	Dummy for callable bonds (=1)
Duration	Duration of the bond at the day of the trade
Age	Time since issuance in years
Relative Trade Size	(Traded nominal value / Amount Outstanding) * 100
Rating AA	Dummy (=1) for AA-rated bonds
Rating A	Dummy (=1) for A-rated bonds
Rating BBB	Dummy (=1) for BBB-rated bonds
Market Capitalization	Market Capitalization of the issuer in billion euro if the issuer is exchange traded
Active Dealers	Number of dealers with non-obsolete quotes before the trade
Volume Bund Futures	Cumulated contract value in billion euro traded in the 30 minutes before the trade
Momentum Bund Futures	Return of the Bund futures contract with shortest time to maturity in basis points in the 30 minutes before the trade. It is multiplied with –1 if the trade was a sell.
Medium	Dummy (=1) if the trade is conducted by one of the four medium sized managers regarding assets under management
Large	Dummy (=1) if the trade is conducted by one of the three largest managers regarding assets under management

Using trade, bond, and issuer characteristics as well as current market conditions to explain the price impact of a trade leads to a very good explanatory power with an adjusted R^2 of 9.66%. Previous studies usually obtain R^2–numbers between 3.5% and 6.3%. The result for our base model is shown in the first column of Table 4.6. We exclude the market capitalization from this model since not all issuers are publicly traded. The first set of variables represents the bond and trade characteristics. Considering the results from column (I), we find callable bonds to be significantly cheaper to trade than non-callable bonds. The price impact for callable bonds is 3.4 bp lower than for non-callable corporate bonds. This result is in line with the results of Edwards, Harris, and Piwowar (2004), who find bonds with an attached put and bonds with an attached call cheaper to trade.[171] Only if trades get very large in their study (representative trade size of $ 1 million), callable bonds are slightly more expensive to trade than straight bonds. They argue that, during the observation period in 2003, yields were very low. Consequently, investors expected many callable bonds to be called soon. As a result, callable bonds should behave more like short-term bonds. Since our data was collected at the end of 2003, the same relation could hold for our sample.

In contrast to the existing literature, we find that the liquidity variables duration and age do not have a significant influence on the price impact of a trade. In turn, the relative trade size has a positive effect on the price impact, significant on a 1% level. The result supports our hypothesis that it is more expensive to trade a larger fraction of the amount outstanding. With each one percent increase in the relative trade size, transaction costs increase by 6.3 bp. Keeping all other factors constant, trading euro 20 million in a bond with an amount outstanding euro 1 billion is 6.3 bp more expensive than trading euro 10 million in the same bond. To confirm our findings, we have also conducted the analysis with separated variables for the amount outstanding and the trade size. The results are shown in Table A.4.1 of the appendix to this chapter. We find the trade size to be positive and significant, while the amount outstanding has a negative and significant influence on the price impact. The results for the amount outstanding are generally in line with the existing literature on corporate bond markets. Edwards, Harris and Piwowar (2004) find a negative relation between the size of the issue and the percentage transaction costs. Only Chakravarty and Sarkar (2003) find the amount outstanding has no significant impact on the effective spread of corporate bonds. Our result contradicts the findings of Schultz (2001) and Edwards, Harris and Piwowar (2004), who find the trade size to be negatively related to the trading costs.[172]

---

171 See and Edwards, Harris, and Piwowar (2004), p. 21.

172 See Schultz (2001), pp. 692-693 and p. 696, Chakravarty and Sarkar (2003), p. 44, and Edwards, Harris and Piwowar (2004), pp. 15-16, p. 18, and p. 21.

Figure 4.3 confirms the economic significance of the relative trading volume for the price impact of European corporate bonds. It is based on the regression results in column (I) of Table 4.6 and shows the price impact depending on trade size and amount outstanding for A-rated non-callable corporate bonds, holding all other variables constant at their sample mean. The trade size and the amount outstanding, for which the price impact is shown, cover the whole range of values observed in our sample. The estimated price impact for an average trade with euro 2.5 million nominal value in a bond with euro 0.75 billion amount outstanding and therefore a relative trade size of 0.34%, is about 4.9 bp, whereas the estimated price impact for the same trade in a bond with an amount outstanding of euro 4.5 billion – the largest amount outstanding in our sample - is only about 3.2 bp. The absolute difference in the price impact becomes larger for larger trades. For a trade size of euro 10 million in a non-callable bond with euro 0.75 billion amount outstanding, the estimated price impact is 11.2 bp, while it is only 4.2 bp for a bond with euro 4.5 billion amount outstanding.

In contrast to the findings of Chakravarty and Sarkar (2003) and Edwards, Harris, and Piwowar (2004), who find increasing spreads for worse credit ratings, we cannot find differences in the price impact for trades in bonds with different default probabilities.[173]

---

[173] See Chakravarty and Sarkar (2003), p. 44 and Edwards, Harris, and Piwowar (2004), p. 23.

Table 4.6: Regression Results for the Price Impact Based on Average Quotes

This table exhibits the result from the estimation of the following regression model:

$$PI_i = \beta_0 + \beta_1 \cdot Callable + \beta_2 \cdot Duration + \beta_3 \cdot Age + \beta_4 \cdot Relative\,Trade\,Size + \beta_5 \cdot Rating\,AA + \beta_6 \cdot Rating\,A + \beta_7 \cdot Rating\,BBB + \beta_8 \cdot Market\,Capitalization + \beta_9 \cdot Active\,Dealers + \beta_{10} \cdot Volume\,Bund\,Future + \beta_{11} \cdot Momentum\,Bund\,Future + \beta_{12} \cdot Medium\,Manager + \beta_{13} \cdot Large\,Manager + \beta_{14} \cdot Momentum\,Bund\,Future * Volume\,Bund\,Future + \varepsilon_i .$$

The price impact is calculated as $PI_{i,t} = \frac{(P_{i,t} - Midquote_{i,t-1})}{Midquote_{i,t-1}} \times S$, whereas the midquote is based on the prevailing average bid- and average ask-quote in the minute before the trade. All return and volume variables are based on the 30-minute interval prior to the trade. In the specification in the first column, we exclude the market capitalization as explanatory variable since not all issuers are public. In the specification in column (II), the market capitalization is included. This reduces our sample size from 1,094 trades to 1,068 trades. The standard errors used to calculate the t-statistics are obtained using White (1980)'s heteroscedasticity-consistent covariance matrix.

Total	**Coefficient Estimates**			**T Statistics**		
	(I)	**(II)**	**(III)**	**(I)**	**(II)**	**(III)**
Intercept	0.6416	-1.5451	3.4118	0.2363	-0.4339	1.6089
Callable	-3.3656	-3.4838	-2.8608	-3.1082	-3.1787	-2.6918
Duration	0.0969	0.0858	0.0636	0.5909	0.5111	0.3799
Age	-0.5474	-0.5145	-0.6155	-1.5851	-1.4378	-1.7594
Relative Trade Size	6.2928	6.006	6.0619	5.3814	5.1914	5.0971
Rating AA	2.8282	4.5904	1.9487	1.173	1.5741	0.9088
Rating A	2.7938	4.2748	1.7576	1.3525	1.6062	1.0469
Rating BBB	2.3143	3.7604	1.3508	1.1107	1.3498	0.7986
Market Cap (bn. euro)		0.0008			0.0781	
Active Dealers	-0.1635	-0.183		-1.2578	-1.3701	
Volume Bund Futures (bn. euro)	0.5838	0.6502		3.6429	3.9704	
Momentum Bund Futures	0.0735	0.0826		1.2065	1.3296	
Medium	-0.8694	-0.2479	-0.5885	-0.7859	-0.2268	-0.5149
Large	-3.1113	-2.3759	-3.2916	-3.0279	-2.3747	-3.2479
Momentum Bund Futures * Volume Bund Futures	-0.0301	-0.0316		-3.1591	-3.2724	
Adjusted R2	0.0966	0.0992	0.0335			
F-statistic	5.5627	4.9682	5.2743			
Prob(F-statistic)	<.0001	<.0001	<.0001			
N	1,094	1,068	1,094			

Figure 4.3: Price Impact by Trading Volume and Amount Outstanding for Non-Callable A-Rated Bonds

This figure plots the estimated price impact for the whole range of nominal trade sizes and amount outstanding in our sample. The figure is based on the results in column (I) of Table 4.6. The results are plotted for trades in non-callable A-rated bonds. All other variables are held constant at their sample mean.

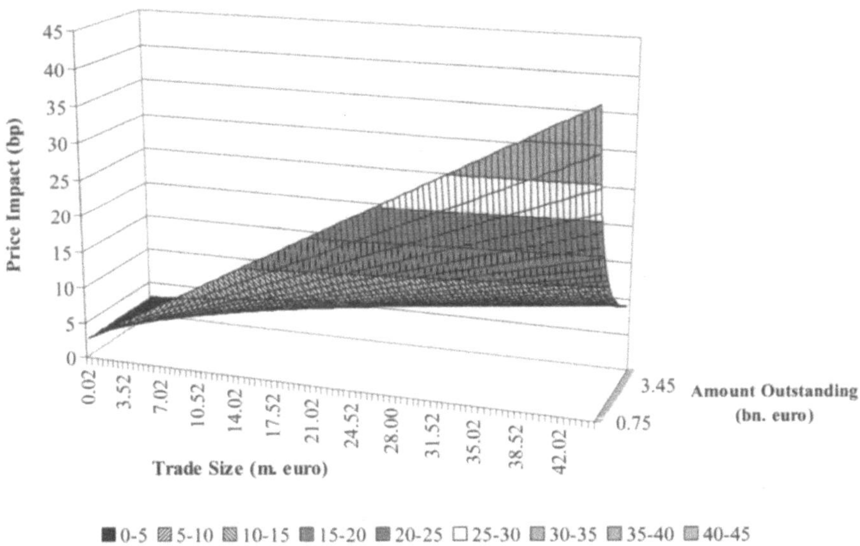

The next set of variables represents the market conditions. The number of active dealers at the time of the trade has no significant impact and, therefore, the hypothesis that a higher competition at the time of the trade has an influence on the price impact cannot be confirmed. The coefficient for the volume traded in the Bund futures contract in the 30 minutes before the trade is highly significant. On the other hand, the coefficients for the return of the Bund futures contract in the 30 minutes before the trade is positive, as expected, but insignificant. The coefficient on the interaction term between the volume of the Bund futures contract and the return of the Bund futures contract is negative and significant. The significance of the coefficients on the volume in the Bund futures contract and on the interaction term confirms the findings of Schultz (2001) that government bonds, and therefore expectations on future inflation, have an impact on corporate bond prices. The influence of the volume and the momentum of the Bund futures contract on the price impact are shown in Figure 4.4. Remember that the returns are multiplied by –1 for sells. As can be seen in Figure 4.4 the impact of the trading volume depends on the sign of the return, or in other words, depends on whether the price of the Bund futures contract moves in the direction of the trade or in the opposite direction of the trade. If the Bund futures return is positive (negative), or equivalently, if the price of the Bund futures contract increases (decreases) for buys (sells), a higher trading volume reduces the price impact and the costs of trading are lower when the price changes of the market are accompanied by high trading volume. In this case, a dealer's risk of holding unwanted inventory is probably lower than in the case of large price movements without reasonable turnover. Surprisingly, negative returns in the Bund futures contract accompanied with high trading volume lead to a higher price impact.

The next two variables represent the characteristics of the asset managers. While medium-sized asset managers have no significant cost advantage compared to small asset managers, the price impact of large asset managers is on average 3.1 bp lower compared to small institutions. This indicates an important effect of the manager's identity. It is plausible that larger managers face lower costs since they regularly trade larger volumes and, therefore, are more important customers for a dealer. We also know from the literature on foreign exchange markets that order flow and price changes are positively related.[174] The information content of the order flow of large customers might therefore be more important for the dealer. This again provides an incentive for the dealer to offer better execution prices to the customer. The result is in line with Schultz (2001), who provides evidence that inactive institutions pay much more to trade corporate bonds than the most active ones. He argues that collecting quotes in such intransparent markets is expensive and time-consuming and that active institutions acquire information as result of their frequent trading.[175]

---

174 See for example Evans and Lyons (2002).
175 See Schultz (2001), pp. 695-697.

Figure 4.4: Price Impact by Bund Futures Momentum and Volume Traded in the Bund Futures Contract for Non-Callable A-Rated Bonds

This figure plots the estimated price impact for the whole range of Bund futures returns and trading volume in the Bund futures. The figure is based on the results in column (I) of Table 4.6. The results are plotted for trades in non-callable A-rated bonds. All other variables are held constant at their sample mean.

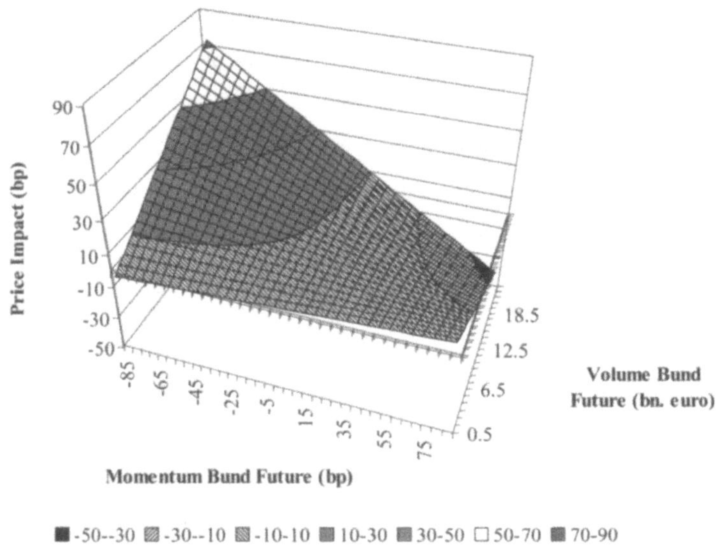

The specification shown in column (II) differs only slightly from column (I). We added the market capitalization of the issuer as explanatory variable. The number of observations reduces by 26 trades to 1,068 observations because some issuers are private companies. However, the coefficient for the market capitalization of the issuer is insignificant and the size of the issuer appears to have no effect on the costs of trading corporate bonds. The sign as well as the significance of the coefficients on the other explanatory variables do not change. We observe almost no change in the marginal effects of the different variables. The adjusted R^2 of 9.92% for this specification is almost the same as for the model in column (I).

In column (III), we drop the variables representing the current market conditions. Even after dropping these variables, the signs and significance of the bond, trade, and issuer characteristics remain almost the same. The age of the bond turns out to be significant on a 10%-level instead of being insignificant in the previous 2 models. The negative sign contradicts the findings of Hong and Warga (2000), Chakravarty and Sarkar (2003), and Edwards, Harris, and Piwowar (2004).[176] Since bond age is insignificant in the models including the current market conditions as explanatory variables, the negative impact of the age of a bond is not very robust. The result of omitting the market conditions is a sharp decline in the adjusted R^2 of the model. With 3.35%, it is in line with the existing literature. This strengthens our finding that the effects of current market conditions are important for the costs of trading. In order to optimize trading costs, this should be taken into account by investors for timing their trades.

4.7.2 *Robustness Checks*

To make sure that the results are not driven by the fact that we use the average bid- and the average ask-quote to determine the midprice, we run the regression using a sub-sample of trades, with positive quoted inside spread before the trade. The calculation of the midquote is then based on the best bid- and best ask-price. Using this restriction, the sample size decreases to 870 trades due to negative inside spreads. The results are shown in Table 4.7. They are qualitatively similar to the results from the full sample in Table 4.6. Signs and significances remain the same, and the change in the level of the coefficients is very small. The adjusted R^2 for all three specifications is also very similar to the adjusted R^2 of the full sample. Overall, our estimator for the unperturbed fair price of the bond is very robust.

---

176 See Hong and Warga (2000), pp. 38-39, Chakravarty and Sarkar (2003), p. 44, and Edwards, Harris, and Piwowar (2004), p.20.

Table 4.7: Regression Results for the Price Impact Based on the Best Bid- and Ask-Quote

This table shows the results of our first robustness test estimating the following regression model:

$$PI_i = \beta_0 + \beta_1 \cdot Callable + \beta_2 \cdot Duration + \beta_3 \cdot Age + \beta_4 \cdot Relative\ Trade\ Size + \beta_5 \cdot Rating\ AA + \beta_6 \cdot Rating\ A + \beta_7 \cdot Rating\ BBB + \beta_8 \cdot Market\ Capitalization + \beta_9 \cdot Active\ Dealers + \beta_{10} \cdot Volume\ Bund\ Future + \beta_{11} \cdot Momentum\ Bund\ Future + \beta_{12} \cdot Medium\ Manager + \beta_{13} \cdot Large\ Manager + \beta_{14} \cdot Momentum\ Bund\ Future * Volume\ Bund\ Future + \varepsilon_i .$$

The price impact is calculated as $PI_{i,t} = \frac{(P_{i,t} - Midquote_{i,t-1})}{Midquote_{i,t-1}} \times S$, whereas the midquote is based on the prevailing best bid- and best ask-quote in the minute before the trade. All return and volume variables are based on the 30-minute interval prior to the trade. Only trades with positive quoted inside spread at least once in the five one-minute intervals prior to the trade are used. The midquote is calculated using the best bid- and the best ask-price. Since negative inside spreads occur very frequently, the sample size reduces to 870 trades excluding the market capitalization from the model and 860 trades including market capitalization. The standard errors used to calculate the t-statistics are obtained using White (1980)'s heteroscedasticity-consistent covariance matrix.

Total	**Coefficient Estimates**			**T Statistics**		
	(I)	**(II)**	**(III)**	**(I)**	**(II)**	**(III)**
Intercept	1.6482	-2.4859	2.2836	0.5912	-0.6482	0.9467
Callable	-2.7146	-2.7411	-2.3841	-2.2656	-2.2583	-2.0344
Duration	0.2259	0.2293	0.1971	1.1598	1.1498	1.0159
Age	-0.2821	-0.1974	-0.3132	-0.7701	-0.5193	-0.8485
Relative Trade Size	6.6096	6.3471	6.5458	4.5623	4.3995	4.514
Rating AA	0.4667	3.1679	1.1063	0.2002	1.1062	0.4393
Rating A	0.4542	3.4276	0.747	0.2378	1.3006	0.3834
Rating BBB	0.2975	3.2442	0.4581	0.1509	1.1415	0.2317
Market Cap (bn. euro)		0.0083			0.7334	
Active Dealers	-0.1925	-0.1924		-1.3417	-1.3119	
Volume Bund Futures (bn. euro)	0.5004	0.5701		2.6923	2.9786	
Momentum Bund Futures	0.0852	0.1003		1.3212	1.5606	
Medium	-0.462	-0.0012	-0.0565	-0.377	-0.001	-0.0448
Large	-2.7727	-2.1263	-2.7367	-2.4544	-1.9203	-2.4864
Momentum Bund Futures * Volume Bund Futures	-0.0381	-0.0411		-3.0996	-3.2982	
Adjusted R2	0.0984	0.1015	0.0314			
F-statistic	4.1492	3.7809	3.4300			
Prob(F-statistic)	<.0001	<.0001	0.0004			
N	870	860	870			

Table 4.8: Regression Results for the Sample without Trades in Callable Bonds

This table shows the results of our second robustness test estimating the following regression model:

$$PI_i = \beta_0 + \beta_1 \cdot Duration + \beta_2 \cdot Age + \beta_3 \cdot Relative\,Trade\,Size + \beta_4 \cdot Rating\,AA + \beta_5 \cdot Rating\,A + \beta_6 \cdot Rating\,BBB + \beta_7 \cdot Market\,Capitalization + \beta_8 \cdot Active\,Dealers + \beta_9 \cdot Volume\,Bund\,Future + \beta_{10} \cdot Momentum\,Bund\,Future + \beta_{11} \cdot Medium\,Manager + \beta_{12} \cdot Large\,Manager + \beta_{13} \cdot Momentum\,Bund\,Future * Volume\,Bund\,Future + \varepsilon_i .$$

The price impact is calculated as $PI_{i,t} = \frac{(P_{i,t} - Midquote_{i,t-1})}{Midquote_{i,t-1}} \times S$, whereas the midquote is based on the prevailing average bid- and average ask-quote in the minute before the trade. All return and volume variables are based on the 30-minute interval prior to the trade. Only trades in non-callable bonds are used in the regression analysis. The exclusion of trades in callable bonds reduces the sample size to 918 institutional trades. The price impact is based on the midquote that is calculated using average bid- and ask-quotes. The standard errors used to calculate the t-statistics are obtained using White (1980)'s heteroscedasticity-consistent covariance matrix.

Total	**Coefficient Estimates**			**T Statistics**		
	(I)	**(II)**	**(III)**	**(I)**	**(II)**	**(III)**
Intercept	-0.4653	-3.0045	2.6901	-0.1598	-0.7725	1.1587
Duration	0.266	0.2549	0.2087	1.1131	1.0373	0.8657
Age	-0.5674	-0.5311	-0.6478	-1.5783	-1.4288	-1.7872
Relative Trade Size (Trade Size*100/Amount Outstanding)	6.5403	6.1627	6.3342	4.7335	4.5066	4.4897
Rating AA	3.0145	4.9937	2.05	1.2058	1.5383	0.9206
Rating A	3.0229	4.7094	1.863	1.4335	1.6475	1.1086
Rating BBB	2.3162	3.9928	1.2208	1.0989	1.3528	0.7303
Market Cap (bn. euro)		0.0021			0.1888	
Active Dealers	-0.2112	-0.2341		-1.4324	-1.5274	
Volume Bund Futures (bn. euro)	0.6876	0.7734		3.7339	4.1016	
Momentum Bund Futures	0.0692	0.0782		1.0878	1.2072	
Medium	-0.7399	-0.0961	-0.4561	-0.6406	-0.0835	-0.3812
Large	-3.2532	-2.4465	-3.4839	-3.0375	-2.3446	-3.3142
Momentum Bund Futures * Volume Bund Futures	-0.0301	-0.0317		-3.096	-3.2209	
Adjusted R2	0.1079	0.1120	0.0312			
F-statistic	5.2927	4.7032	4.8273			
Prob(F-statistic)	<.0001	<.0001	<.0001			
N	918	892	918			

For the next robustness check, we exclude all callable bonds from our sample. Talks with some of the asset managers revealed that, for callable bonds, the time to the next call date is more important to them than the time to maturity. It is thus plausible that callable bonds behave more like bonds whose time to maturity equals the time to next call date. If the slopes are different for callable and non-callable bonds, this might explain why especially the coefficient of the duration is insignificant in our regression results. Table 4.8 exhibits the results for sample without trades in callable bonds. The sample size reduces to 918 trades in non-callable bonds. Once more, we find signs and significances of the variables to be very similar to the full sample. The changes in the slopes are again very small, indicating that the difference between callable and non-callable bonds is captured well by our dummy variable.

4.8 The Costs of Trading Corporate Bonds and Stocks – A Comparison

It is still an open question whether corporate bonds or stocks are more expensive to trade (for a given trade size) and whether the difference in trading costs is large enough to influence the weights attributed to stocks and corporate bonds in a portfolio. If the difference in the cost of trading bonds and stocks is high, an investor has to adjust his expectations in the raw return by the different costs of trading bonds and stocks. This might lead to different investment decisions or a different composition of the investors' portfolio.

To address this topic, we compare the costs of trading European corporate bonds with the costs of trading the stocks of the same issuers. For this analysis, we use a sub-sample of all trades in corporate bonds issued by a Stoxx 600-company. The Stoxx 600 is an equity index that comprises the 600 largest European companies in terms of free float adjusted market capitalization. We use a sample of equity trades collected by alpha portfolio advisors GmbH between February and April 2003. Both trade datasets have a comparable structure. Ten asset managers reported equity trades in Stoxx 600-companies with exact time stamp.[177] At the same time, tick-by-tick bid- and ask-quotes were collected from Reuters. The quotes are collected from the exchange with the

[177] Three of the asset managers took part in both the bond and the equity project.

largest trading volume in each stock. In contrast to bond markets, the quotes are executable.

We compare the trading costs of the most liquid euro-denominated corporate bonds with the trading costs of the most liquid European stocks. Both segments represent a large fraction of the market capitalization / amount outstanding of the European corporate debt and equity markets. Even though the asset managers reported overall more than 10,000 equity trades analyzed in the project, the asset managers traded only 379 different stocks during our three-month observation period. Out of the 379 stocks, the stocks traded less than 10 times had an average free float market capitalization of euro 2 billion, The stocks traded 10 times or more but less than 100 times have an average free float market capitalization of euro 7 billion, and those traded more often than 100 times had an average free float market capitalization of euro 29 billion. Most of the asset managers trading takes place in the highly liquid segment and emphasizes the importance of the large cap segment for the overall dollar costs of trading stocks.

The matching procedure reduces the sample of corporate bond transactions to 770 trades. Even though one AAA-rated bond remains in our sample, the asset managers did not trade this bond during our observation period. Table 4.9 gives a short overview on the matched sample of equity trades. We observe trades in 61 different companies that issued at least one of the above-analyzed 211 bonds. The market capitalization of these 61 companies was euro 1,616 billion at the beginning of the observation period. In total, the data contains 2,687 equity trades.[178] Seven out of the ten participating asset managers traded at least one of the 61 different stocks. The market value of all trades is euro 1.7 billion. The average trade size is euro 0.63 million – less than a fourth of the average trade size for corporate bonds. Buys are slightly smaller than sells.

---

[178] We sometimes observe multiple trades by the same asset manager in the same stock at the same time using different brokers. These transactions are aggregated to one trade.

Table 4.9: Descriptive Statistics of the Matched Institutional Equity Trades

This table provides an overview on the sample of trades in stocks issued by the companies that have bonds outstanding.

Trade and Quote Data	All Trades	Buys	Sells
Number of Trades	2,687	984	1,703
% of trades	*100%*	*36.62%*	*63.38%*
Number of Different Stocks	61	55	58
Market Value all Trades (billion euro)	1.6959	0.5687	1.1272
Avg. Trade Size (million euro)	0.6311	0.57809	0.6619
Number of Active Managers	7	7	7

Table 4.10 compares the value-weighted costs of trading corporate bonds to the value weighted costs of trading stocks. The first column exhibits the price impact of trading corporate bonds. The total price impact is 0.1 bp lower for this sub-sample than for the full sample. Due to the different market structures of bond and equity markets, we calculate two different cost measures for equities. All trades in the corporate bond markets are principal trades, while most of the trades in equity markets are agency trades. For an agency trade, the customer usually has to pay a commission to the broker. Other fees or taxes like the stamp duty in the U.K. and Switzerland are charged on some exchanges. These costs have to be added to the price impact to make the costs of trading equities comparable to the costs of trading corporate bonds. Our data contains exact information on those fees and thence, Table 4.10 exhibits both the price impact of trading stocks and the price impact plus commission and additional fees. The price impact is calculated using the midquote from the best bid- and ask-price at the end of the minute before the order is passed to the broker. Excluding additional fees, we observe a total price impact of 57.13 bp for European equities. Accounting for additional fees, we observe total costs of trading liquid European equities of 69.33 bp. Although we analyze the trading costs of the most liquid market segment exclusively, the average trading costs are higher than 27 German asset managers stated in a survey conducted by Johanning and Schlenger (2002). They estimated trading costs of 62 bp

for active managed portfolios and 32 bp for passive portfolios.[179] Compared with the price impact of trading corporate bonds, equities are much more expensive to trade although we focus on the execution costs for highly liquid stocks. We also have not taken the different trade sizes into account yet, which we observe for the two asset classes.

Table 4.10: Price Impact using Average Bid- and Ask-Prices

This table compares the costs of trading European corporate bonds with the costs of trading stock by the same issuers. The price impact is calculated as $PI_{i,t} = \frac{(P_{i,t} - Midquote_{i,t-1})}{Midquote_{i,t-1}} \times S$, where S is an indicator variable that equals 1 for buys and -1 for sells.
The midquote in the minute before the trade is calculated using average bid- and ask-quotes for corporate bonds and using the best bid- and the best ask-quote for our sample of institutional equity trades. The first column presents the price impact of trading European corporate bonds. The next column presents the price impact of the institutional equity trades and in the last column, broker commission and stamp duty are taken into account. The presented averages are weighted by market value of the trade.

	Bonds	**Stocks** (Commission and Stamp Duty Included)	**Stocks** (Commission and Stamp Duty Excluded)
Mean	5.7069	69.3266	57.1296
std	*0.4593*	*2.2599*	*2.2556*
Median	3.9284	45.3671	30.6704
< euro 0.5m	2.3384	23.7600	11.5091
euro 0.5-5m	3.9553	50.5706	38.9525
euro 5-10m	4.8197	52.0921	39.6966
> euro 10m	7.9439	147.9933	134.7839
N	770	2,691	2,691

[179] See Johanning and Schlenger (2002), p. 94. Compared to the most recent literature on equity trading costs, our results are at the upper end. Chiyachantana et al. (2004) find for developed markets trading costs (implicit and explicit) of 53 bp for the period from January 1997 until march 1998 and 44 bp for the first three quarters in 2001 (the first quarter 2001 for US stocks). Bikker, Spierdijk, and van der Sluis (2004) use trade data from a pension fund. Although their data comprises on average larger trades than our data, they find an average price impact of 19.6 bp for buys and 25.6 bp for sells respectively. See Chiyachantana et al. (2004), p. 884 and Bikker, Spierdijk, and van der Sluis (2004), p. 9.

To account for different average trade sizes, we display trading costs for different size categories. The results are shown in Table 4.10 and Figure 4.5. The numbers above the bars represent the trading costs in basis points. We again exhibit trading costs with and without explicit cost for equities. In the smallest trade size category, the price impact for corporate bonds is 2.3 bp, while the price impact for equities is about 11.5 bp. Accounting for explicit costs, we find the execution costs for stocks to be 23.8 bp. The difference in the cost of trading stocks and bonds becomes much more obvious and important for larger trade size categories. While the costs of trading bonds are on average 4.0 bp for trades with a market value of $ 0.5 million to $ 5 million, the costs of trading stocks are already 39 bp (50.6 bp) when explicit costs are excluded (included). In the largest trade size category for trades larger than $ 10 million, the market impact is on average 7.9 bp for trading corporate bonds and 135 bp for equities respectively. Adding explicit costs, the total costs of trading highly liquid stocks are on average 148 bp during the observation period in our sample.

These results emphasize the economic significance of the existing differences in the costs of trading corporate bonds and stocks. Although we focus our analysis on the most liquid bonds and stocks, the difference is up to 140 bp for the largest trade size category. Investors have to take this difference into account on several levels of their investment process. As a result, the strategic asset allocation is clearly affected. After accounting for the excess trading costs for equities, the weight attributed to corporate bonds is higher compared to the weight of equities. Furthermore, the difference in trading costs is even more important for the tactical, medium term oriented asset allocation. Even if the investor takes the correct round trip costs into account, the costs associated with the trading within the different asset classes leads to a decrease in equity returns relative to bond returns.

Figure 4.5: The Costs of Trading Stocks and Corporate Bonds for Different Trade Size Categories – A Comparison

This figure compares the costs of trading European corporate bonds and European equities by trade size category. The price impact is calculated as $PI_{i,t}^{temp} = \frac{(P_{i,t} - Midquote_{i,close})}{Midquote_{i,t-1}} \times S$.

The midquote in the minute before the trade is calculated using average bid- and ask-quotes for corporate bonds and using the best bid- and the best ask-quote for our sample of institutional equity trades. For European stocks, we report the price impact, as well as the price impact plus broker commission and stamp duty.

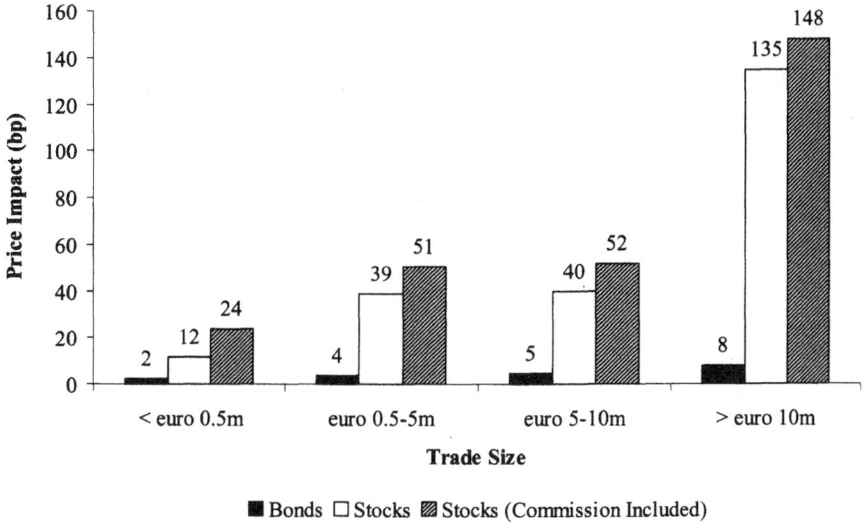

4.9 Conclusion

In this article, we analyze the costs of trading euro-denominated corporate bonds. In contrast to the existing literature, we use indicative quotes on a tick-by-tick basis to directly calculate the prevailing midquote before the trade. In this way, we do not have to rely on daily effective spreads or estimate the fair price using a factor model. This avoids potential biases in the measurement of the price impact. Using a sample of 1,094 institutional trades in euro-denominated corporate bonds collected during 62 trading days from September until December 2003, we find trading costs of 5.60 bp. With 5.12 bp, buys are slightly less expensive than sells with 5.96 bp.

To explain the price impact of trades in euro-denominated corporate bonds we include the same liquidity variables typically used in previous studies of US corporate bond markets. We also account for the market conditions in the 30 minutes before the trade in our regression model. The relative trade size has a strong positive effect on the price impact and callable bonds are significantly cheaper to trade than non-callable bonds. Surprisingly, many of the liquidity variables like age, duration, rating, and market capitalization of the issuer do not have a significant impact on the costs of trading euro-denominated corporate bonds. We confirm the hypothesis that the market conditions in the 30 minutes before the trade significantly influence the costs of trading corporate bonds. The volume in the Bund futures contract as a proxy for new information arrival has a positive effect on the price impact and the interaction term for the volume and the return in the Bund futures has a significant negative impact on the costs of trading. The number of active dealers, on the other hand, does not influence transaction costs significantly. In addition, our sample provides evidence that large buy-side customers transact more cheaply than smaller asset managers. A comparison with equity trades in highly liquid stocks shows, that the costs of trading corporate bonds are only $1/10^{th}$ to $1/20^{th}$ of the costs of trading stocks of the same issuer.

As a whole, the costs of trading euro-denominated corporate bonds are comparable to costs at the US$ market after the introduction of TRACE. This result is remarkable since the euro-denominated market is smaller and less transparent than the market for US$ corporate bonds. The costs are mainly determined by the relative trade size and the market conditions before the trade. If immediacy is not a critical factor to a specific transaction, the timing of the trade is definitely a determinant that can be influenced by investors. Investors also have to adjust expected returns by the costs of trading bonds and stocks when they determine the portfolio weights of different asset classes. Neglecting the difference in trading costs may lead to an overestimation of the expected excess returns of equities relative to corporate bonds. As a result, the weight attributed to stocks is too large. Hence, the realized portfolio might not be optimal for an institutional investor.

Appendix to Part 4

Table A.4.1: Regression Results with Trading Volume and Amount Outstanding as Separate Independent Variables

This table exhibits the result from the estimation of the following regression model:

$$PI_i = \beta_0 + \beta_1 \cdot Callable + \beta_2 \cdot Duration + \beta_3 \cdot Age + \beta_4 \cdot Nominal\ Trading\ Volume + \beta_6 \cdot Rating\ AA + \beta_7 \cdot Rating\ A + \beta_8 \cdot Rating\ BBB + \beta_9 \cdot Market\ Capitalization + \beta_{10} \cdot Active\ Dealers + \beta_{11} \cdot Volume\ Bund\ Future + \beta_{12} \cdot Momentum\ Bund\ Future + \beta_{13} \cdot Medium\ Manager + \beta_{14} \cdot Large\ Manager + \beta_{15} \cdot Momentum\ Bund\ Future * Volume\ Bund\ Future + \varepsilon_i .$$

The price impact is calculated as $PI_{i,t} = \frac{(P_{i,t} - Midquote_{i,t-1})}{Midquote_{i,t-1}} \times S$, whereas the midquote is based on the prevailing average bid- and average ask-quote in the minute before the trade. All return and volume variables are based on the 30-minute interval prior to the trade. In the specification in the first column, we exclude the market capitalization as explanatory variable since not all issuers are public. In the specification in column (II), the market capitalization is included. This reduces our sample size from 1,094 trades to 1,068 trades. The standard errors used to calculate the t-statistics are obtained using White (1980)'s heteroscedasticity-consistent covariance matrix.

Total	Coefficient Estimates			T Statistics		
	(I)	(II)	(III)	(I)	(II)	(III)
Intercept	2.1672	-0.6643	4.8763	0.7778	-0.1856	2.1627
Callable	-3.3504	-3.4519	-2.8592	-3.1678	-3.2233	-2.7453
Duration	0.0899	0.0812	0.0577	0.5505	0.4848	0.3441
Age	-0.5367	-0.5	-0.6038	-1.553	-1.3974	-1.7242
Nominal Trading Volume (m. euro)	0.4292	0.4067	0.4111	4.4573	4.249	4.1869
Amount Outstanding (bn. euro)	-0.9638	-0.9603	-0.9377	-2.8325	-2.801	-2.6092
Rating AA	2.6397	4.8488	1.7698	1.0861	1.6538	0.8147
Rating A	2.8408	4.848	1.8089	1.363	1.791	1.0585
Rating BBB	2.6236	4.5911	1.6682	1.2494	1.6172	0.9712
Market Cap (bn. euro)		0.0027			0.2673	
Active Dealers	-0.156	-0.172		-1.1884	-1.2744	
Volume Bund Futures (bn. euro)	0.5694	0.6369		3.5574	3.9005	
Momentum Bund Futures	0.0741	0.0830		1.2173	1.3411	
Medium	-0.7156	-0.088	-0.4414	-0.6417	-0.0801	-0.3844
Large	-2.8779	-2.1323	-3.0604	-2.7806	-2.1204	-3.0034
Momentum Bund Futures * Volume Bund Futures	-0.0304	-0.032		-3.1869	-3.3073	
Adjusted R2	0.0899	0.0930	0.0271			
F-statistic	4.9002	4.3994	4.3628			
Prob(F-statistic)	0.0000	0.0000	0.0000			
N	1,094	1,068	1,094			

5 Summary, Conclusion, and Further Research

5.1 Summary and Conclusions

This thesis contains three parts of empirical research on the microstructure of bond markets that are related to the organizational structure as well as the price formation and the cost of liquidity in bond markets.

Part 2 analyzes for the first time the phenomenon of the coexistence of several trading segments in the interdealer as well as the customer-dealer market. In the secondary market for German federal securities, we observe over decades grown on- and off-exchange market structures and raise the question whether these can be justified economically, or whether manifested institutional conditions conserve the historically grown market structure. The three existing parallel trading segments – exchange trading, bilateral OTC trading, and brokered OTC trading – exhibit substantial differences regarding the price formation mechanism and the anonymity of the counterparties. Therefore our initial hypothesis is that each trading mechanism fulfills its own function for the market participants and attracts different transaction desires. We obtain significant empirical results, indicating that the three different trading possibilities are not seen as interchangeable trading segments by the market participants. Instead, each secondary market segment satisfies different transaction needs. In summary, our analysis shows that the prevailing structure of the secondary market for German federal securities with several differently organized trading segments is justified on the basis of economic considerations. Institutional conditions do not seem to be the main cause for the existence of the different trading segments.

For the interdealer market for German federal securities it can be assumed that, in future, the proportion of bilateral OTC transactions will still continue to increase, particularly debited to the brokered OTC transactions. This is because of the progressive development and dissemination of electronic trading systems. The forecasted loss of the importance of independent brokers working on a commission basis relies on the observation that electronic trading systems exist in the interdealer market in the meantime, which make an anonymous bilateral trade for the market participants possible. Since they have also lost a crucial competitive advantage with the loss of the unique position as anonymity provider, we assume it already came to a reduction of the brokered OTC trades and this development will continue.

The potential of the exchange trading is limited to transactions with low absolute trading volumes due to its organization as auction market. Higher trade volumes at the exchange might primarily be the result of the activities of the German Bundesbank traditionally implemented over the German exchanges. Without the daily market management operations and the resulting daily exchange trading of the German Bundesbank as a contractor for institutional market participants, exchange members would presumably use the exchange floor only as a trading platform for retail orders and institutional transactions with very small trade volume.

The third part of the thesis studies the short-run price dynamics between the interdealer market and the customer-dealer market. The sample comprises euro benchmark government bonds traded on EuroMTS. Thereby, the focus is on two questions. Which market contributes more to the price discovery? Is the share of the price contribution related to security characteristics? Hasbrouck's (1996, 2003) information share approach is applied to a unique integrated dataset containing quotes from EuroMTS as well as quotes for a representative sample of dealers from the customer-dealer market.

In contradiction to the commonly held belief that the interdealer market slightly leads the customer-dealer market,[180] we find EuroMTS' share in the price discovery process for benchmark government bonds is dominated by the customer-dealer market. We also provide evidence that the information share of EuroMTS is larger for illiquid bonds than for liquid bonds. Especially the number of quote changes and the percentage of crossed and locked quotes have a significant impact on the interdealer market's information share. Nevertheless, we also find that the customer-dealer market is the dominant market for almost all of the bonds in our sample.

The results also suggest that, especially for very liquid bonds, the pricing error is smaller in the customer-dealer market. Although the customer-dealer sphere is more decentralized, collecting information from a sample of dealers from the customer-dealer market helps investors to avoid pricing errors. Conversely, our findings indicate that for less liquid bonds, EuroMTS may be the more dominant market. This supports the conclusion of Gravelle (2002). He emphasizes that the prevailing multiple-dealer

180 See, e.g., Lyons (2001), p. 115.

structure in government bond markets is especially suited for illiquid securities when the volume of an individual trade is still very large.[181]

Part 4 analyzes the cost of liquidity in euro corporate bond markets. Unlike other studies that impute trading costs from trade prices alone, these costs are measured directly using quotations from multiple dealers prior to the trade. Trading costs are about 5.60 bp, whereas buys with 5.12 bp are slightly less expensive than sells with 5.96 bp. Regression analysis provides evidence that callable bonds are cheaper to trade and that the relative trade size as well as the current market conditions in the 30 minutes before a trade significantly influence the cost of trading euro corporate bonds. Additionally, our sample provides evidence that large buy-side customers transact more cheaply than smaller asset managers. A comparison with equity trades in highly liquid stocks shows that the costs of trading corporate bonds are roughly a little less than 10% of the costs of trading stocks of the same issuer.

In general, the smaller size and the opaqueness of the euro corporate bond market relative to the US market do not translate into higher costs of trading. Investors also have to adjust expected returns by the costs of trading bonds and stocks when they determine the optimal portfolio weights of the two asset classes. Neglecting the difference in trading costs may lead to an overestimation of the expected excess returns for equities relative to corporate bonds. As a result, the weight attributed to stocks is too large. Therefore, the realized portfolio might not be optimal for an institutional investor.

5.2 Further Research

Based on the prevailing findings, there are several directions for future research. The analyses were conducted with a sample of very liquid investment grade bonds with a large amount outstanding. The results in Part 3 already suggest that some of the findings may be different for less liquid bonds. Based on the findings of Part 2 for the organizational structure of bond markets, brokered interdealer trading may be much more important for illiquid securities than liquid securities since order flow information is of even greater value. Less liquid bonds have been, e.g., traded on NewEuroMTS

181 See Section 4.8 where the institutional trade sizes for corporate bonds and equities are compared, as well as Gravelle (2002), pp. 30-32.

since May 1, 2004. They comprise government securities for the 10 new states that entered the EU (European Union).

Besides less liquid government bonds, results for non-investment grade corporate bonds are of great interest for practitioners as well as academicians. They differ from investment grade corporate bonds since private payoff relevant (company-specific) information has a strong impact on the prices of these bonds.[182] One particularly interesting question addresses the costs of trading these bonds. If trading these bonds is still relatively cheap in contrast to trading equity of the same issuer, investors should examine whether investing in corporate bonds instead of equity has a better risk-return profile.

Another issue not addressed here due to limited data availability is the efficiency of different trading platforms within the interdealer environment and within the customer-dealer environment. The Bond Market Association (2005a) provides an excellent overview on the different trading platforms in both markets.[183] The trading methods on these platforms vary strongly. Some of them offer firm quotes or quote requests, while others are based on cross-matching. Unfortunately, an analysis of these platforms may be difficult due to limited access to data.

Moreover, we cannot answer the question how individual dealers behave in the two market spheres in response to transactions in the customer-dealer and the interdealer market respectively. The results may throw some further light on the dealer behavior in multiple-dealership markets and are related to Part 3 of this dissertation. In addition to the result that the customer-dealer market dominates the price discovery process of very liquid euro benchmark bonds than the interdealer market, it is of interest if dealers disseminating price signals in response to a customer trade are responsible for this price leadership. In this case, the quotes of individual dealers may already reveal private information on their customer order flow.

---

182 See, e.g., Schultz (2001), p. 683.
183 See The Bond Market Association (2005a), pp. 7-9.

References

Alexander, G. J., Edwards, A. K., and Ferri, M. G. (2000): The Determinants of Trading Volume of High-Yield Corporate Bonds, in: Journal of Financial Markets, Vol. 3, 177-204.

Almon, S. (1965): The Distributed Lag between Capital Appropriations and Expenditures, Econometrics 33, 178-196.

Amihud, Y., and Mendelson, H. (1991): Liquidity, Maturity, and the Yields on U.S. Treasury Securities, Journal of Finance 46, 1411-1425.

Ates, A. and Wang, G. H. K. (2005): Information Transmission in Electronic versus Open-Outcry Trading Systems: An Analysis of U.S. Equity Index Futures Markets, Journal of Futures Markets 25, 679-715.

Backhaus, K., Erichson, B., Plinke, W., and Weiber, R. (2003): Multivariate Analysemethoden, Berlin.

Baillie, R. T., Booth, G. G., Tse, Y., and Zabotina, T. (2002): Price Discover and Common Factor Models, Journal of Financial Markets 5, 209-321.

Benston, G. J. and Hagerman, R. L. (1974): Determinants of Bid-Asked Spreads in the Over-the-Counter Market, Journal of Financial Economics 1, 353-364.

Bessembinder, H., Maxwell, W., and Venkataraman, K. (2005): Optimal Market Transparency: Evidence from the Initiation of Trade Reporting in Corporate Bonds, Working Paper.

Beveridge, S. and Nelson, C. R. (1981): A New Approach to Decomposition of Time Series in Permanent and Transitory Components with Particular Attention to the Measurement of the "Business Cycle", Journal of Monetary Economics 7, 151-174.

Biais, B., Hillion, P., and Spatt, C. (1999): Price Discovery and Learning during the Preopening Period in the Paris Bourse, Journal of Political Economy 107, 1218-1248.

Biais, B., Glosten, L., and Spatt, C. (2004): The Microstructure of Stock Markets, Working Paper.

Bikker, J. A., Spierdijk, L., and van der Sluis, P. J. (2004): The Implementation Shortfall of Institutional Equity Trades, EFA 2004 Maastricht Meetings Paper No. 1813.

Bloomfield, R. and O'Hara, M. (2000): Can Transparent Markets Survive?, Journal of Financial Economics 55, 425-459.

Bollerslev, T., and Domowitz, I. (1993): Trading Patterns and Prices in the Interbank Foreign Exchange Market, Journal of Finance 48, 1421-1443.

Bollerslev, T. and Melvin, M. (1994): Bid-Ask Spreads and Volatility in the Foreign Exchange Market: An Empirical Analysis, Journal of International Economics, 36, 355-372.

Chan, L. K. C., and Lakonishok, J. (1993): Institutional Trades and Intraday Stock Price Behaviour, Journal of Financial Economics 33, 173-199.

Chan, L. K. C. and Lakonishok, J. (1995): The Behaviour of Stock Prices Around Institutional Trades, Journal of Finance 50, 1147-1174.

Chan, L. K. C. and Lakonishok, J. (1997): Insitutional Equity Trading Costs: NYSE Versus Nasdaq, Journal of Finance 52, 713-735.

Cao, C., Ghysels, E., and Hatheway, F. (2000): Price Discovery without Trading: Evidence from the Nasdaq preopening, Journal of Finance 55, 1339-1365.

Chakravarty, S. and Sarkar, A. (2003): Trading Costs in Three U.S. Bonds Markets, Journal of Fixed Income, 13, 39-48.

Cheung, Y.-W. and Wong, C. Y.-P. (2000): A Survey of Market Practitioners' Views on Exchange Rate Dynamics, Journal of International Economics 51, 401-419.

Chiyachantana, C. N., Jain, P. K., Jiang, C., and Wood, R. A. (2004): International Evidence on Instiutional Trading Behaviour and Price Impact, Journal of Finance 59, 869-898.

Coase, R. H. (1937): The Nature of the Firm, Economica 4, 385-405.

Cohen, K. J., Maier, S. F., Schwartz R. A., and Whitcomb, D. K. (1986): The Microstructure of Securities Markets, Prentice-Hall, Englewood Cliffs.

Commons, J. (1931): Institutional Economics, American Economic Review 21, 648-657.

Dacorogna, M. M., Muller, U. A., Nagler, R. J., Olsen, R. B., and Pictet, O. V. (1993): A Geographical Model for the Daily and Weekly Seasonal Volatility in the Foreign Exchange Market, Journal of International Money and Finance 12, 413-438.

de Jong, F. (2002): Measures of Contributions to Price Discovery: A Comparison, Journal of Financial Markets 5, 323-327.

de Jong, F; Mahieu, R., and Schotman, P. (1998): Price Discovery in the Foreign Exchange Markets: An Empirical Analysis of the yen/dmark rate, Journal of International Money and Finance 17, 5-27.

Demsetz, H. (1968): The Cost of Transacting, Quarterly Journal of Economics 82, 33-53.

Easley, D. and O'Hara, M. (1987): Price, Trade Size, and Information in Securities Markets, Journal of Financial Economics 19, 69-90.

Easley, D., Kiefer, N. M., and O'Hara, M. (1996): Cream-Skimming or Profit-Sharing? The Curious Role of Purchased Order Flow, Journal of Finance 51, 811-831.

Edwards, A. K., Harris, L. E., and Piwowar, M. S. (2004): Corporate Bond Market Transparency and Transaction Costs, Working Paper.

Edwards, M. and Wagner, W. (1993) "Best Execution", Financial Analysts Journal, Vol. 49, 65-71.

Engle, R. F. and Granger, C. W. J. (1987): Co-Integration and Error Correction: Representation, Estimation, and Testing, Econometrica 55, 251-276.

European Central Bank (2004): Monthly Bulletin, May 2004.

European Central Bank (2005): Monthly Bulletin, August 2005.

Evans, M. D. D. (2002): FX Trading and Exchange Rate Dynamics, Journal of Finance 57, 2405-2447.

Evans, M. D. D. and Lyons, R. K. (2002): Order Flow and Exchange Rate Dynamics, Journal of Political Economy 110, 170-180.

Fleming, M. J. and Remolona, E. M. (1999): Price Formation and Liquidity in the U.S. Treasury Market: The Response to Public Information, Journal of Finance 54, 1901-1915.

Floegel, V. and Kesy, C. (2004): Organisation des Sekundärhandels von Bundeswertpapieren: Historisch gewachsen! Ökonomisch begründbar?, Kredit und Kapital 37, 500-536.

Floegel, V., Kesy, C. and Panchapagesan, V. (2005): Institutional Trading Costs in European Corporate Bond Markets, Working Paper.

Flood, M. D., Huisman, R., Koedijk, K. G., and Mahieu R. J. (1999): Quote Disclosure and Price Discovery in Multiple-Dealer Financial Markets, Review of Financial Studies 12, 37-59.

Fong, K., Madhavan, A., and Swan, P. L. (2001): Why do Markets Fragment? A Panel-Data Analysis of Off-Exchange Trading, University of Sydney Business School, Working Paper.

Foster, D. F. and Viswanathan, S. (1993): Variations in Trading Volume, Return Volatility, and Trading Costs: Evidence on Recent Price Formation Models, Journal of Finance 48, 187-211.

Franke, G. and Hess, D. (1998): Anonymous Electronic Trading versus Floor Trading, Working Paper, University of Konstanz.

Garbade, K. D. and Silber, W. L. (1976): Price Dispersion in the Government Securities Market, Journal of Political Economy 84, 721-740.

Gerke, W. and Rasch, S. (1992): Ausgestaltung des Blockhandels an der Börse, Die Bank 4, 193-2001.

Gerke, W., Arneth, S., and Bosch, R. (2000): The Market Maker Privilege in an Experimental Computerised Stock Market, Kredit und Kapital, Special Issue 15, 173-201.

Gerke, W., Arneth, S., and Shya, C. (2000): The Impact of the Order Book-Privilege on Traders' Behavior and the Market Process – An Experimental Investigation, Journal of Economic Psychology 21, 167-189.

German Bundesbank (2000): The Market for German Federal Securities, 3rd edition, Frankfurt/Main.

Gonzalo, J. and Granger, C. W. J. (1995): Estimation of common long-memory components in cointegrated systems, Journal of Business & Economic Statistics 13, 27-36.

Goodhart, C. (1988): The Foreign Exchange Market: A Random Walk with a Dragging Anchor, Economics 55, 437-460.

Gravelle, T. (2002): The Microstructure of Dealership Equity and Government Securities Markets: How They Differ, Working Paper 2002-09, Bank of Canada.

Greene, W. H. (2003): Econometric Analysis, 5th edition, New Jersey.

Grünbichler, A. (1994): Computerbörse versus Präsenzbörse, Financial Markets and Portfolio Management 8, 499-507.

Hamilton, J. D. (1994): Time Series Analysis, Princeton.

Harris, F. H. deB., McInish, T. H., and Wood, R. A. (2002): Security Price Adjustment across Exchanges: An Investigation of Common Factor Components for Dow Stocks, Journal of Financial Markets 5, 277-308.

Harris, L. E., and Piwowar, M. S. (2004): Municipal Bond Liquidity, Working Paper.

Hasbrouck, J. (1993): Assessing the Quality of a Security Market: A New Approach to Transaction-Cost Measurement, Review of Financial Studies 6, 191-212.

Hasbrouck, J. (1995): One Security, Many Markets: Determining the Contributions to Price Discovery, Journal of Finance 50, 1175-1199.

Hasbrouck, J. (2002): Stalking the "Efficient Price" in market microstructure specifications: An Overview, Journal of Financial Markets 5, 239-339.

Hasbrouck, J. (2003): Intraday Price Formation in U.S. Equity Index Markets, Journal of Finance 58, 2375-2399.

Hautsch, N. and Hess, D. (2002): The Processing of Non-Anticipated Information in Financial Markets: Analyzing the Impact of Surprises in the Employment Report, European Finance Review 6, 133-161.

Holthausen, R. W., Leftwich, R. W., and Mayers, D. (1987): The Effect of Large Block Transactions on Security Prices, Journal of Financial Economics 19, 237-267.

Holthausen, R. W., Leftwich, R. W., and Mayers, D. (1990): Large Block Transactions, the Speed of Response, and Temporary and Permanent Stock-Price Effects, Journal of Financial Economics 26, 71-95.

Hong, G. and Warga, A. (2000): An Empirical Study of Bond Market Transactions, Financial Analysts Journal 56, 32-46.

International Organization of Securities Commissions (2004): Transparency of Corporate Bond Markets, May 2004.

Ito, T., Lyons, R. K., and Melvin, M. T. (1998): Is There Private Information in the FX Market? The Tokyo Experiment, Journal of Finance 53, 1111-1130.

Johanning, L. and Schlenger, C. (2002): Best Execution from a German Perspective, in: Best Execution, European Asset Management Association, London.

Keim, D. B. and Madhavan, A. (1997): Transactions Costs and Investment Style: An Inter-Exchange Analysis of Institutional Equity Trades, Journal of Financial Economics 46, 265-292.

Keim, D. B. and Madhavan, A. (1998): The Cost of Institutional Equity Trades, in: Financial Analysts Journal 54, 50-69.

Kesy, C. (2003): Informationsverarbeitung am Rentenmarkt, Bad Soden.

Kofman, P. and Moser, J. T. (1997): Spreads, Information Flows and Transparency across Trading Systems, Applied Financial Economics 7, 281-294.

Krahnen, J. P. (1993): Finanzwirtschaftslehre zwischen Markt und Institution, Die Betriebswirtschaft 53, 793-805.

Kurov, A., and Lasser, D. (2004): Price Dynamics in the Regular and E-mini Futures Markets, Journal of Financial and Quantitative Analysis 39, 365-384.

Kyle, A. (1985): Continuous Auctions and Insider Trading, Econometrica 53, 1315-1235.

Lehmann, B. N. (2002): Some Desiderata for the Measurement of Price Discovery across Markets, Journal of Financial Markets 5, 259-276.

Leland, H. E. (1994): Corporate Debt Value, Bond Covenants, and Optimal Capital Structure, in: Journal of Finance, Vol. 49, 1213-1252.

Lyons, R. K. (1995): Tests of Microstructural Hypotheses in the Foreign Exchange Market, Journal of Financial Economics 39, 321-351.

Lyons, R. K. (1996a): Optimal Transparency in a Dealer Market with an Application to Foreign Exchange Markets, Journal of Financial Intermediation 5, 225-254.

Lyons, R. K. (1996b): Foreign Exchange Volume: Sound and Fury Signifying nothing? in: J. Frankel et al. eds., The Microstructure of Foreign Exchange Markets, Chicago.

Lyons, R. K. (1997): A Simultaneous Trade Model of the Foreign Exchange Hot Potato, Journal of International Economics 42, 275-298.

Lyons, R. K. (2001): The Microstructure Approach to Exchange Rates, Cambridge.

Madhavan, A. (1995): Consolidation, Fragmentation, and the Disclosure of Trading Information, Review of Financial Studies 8, 579-603.

Madhavan, A. (2000): Market Microstructure: A Survey, Journal of Financial Markets 3, 205-259.

Martens, M. (1998): Price Discovery in High and Low Volatility Periods: Open Outcry versus Electronic Trading, Journal of International Financial Markets, Institutions and Money 8, 243-260.

Merton, R. C. (1974): On the Pricing of Corporate Debt: The Risk Structure of Interest Rates, Journal of Finance 29, 449-470.

Milgrom, P. R. and Roberts, M. C. (1992): Economics, Organization, and Management, Englewood Cliffs.

Nabben, S. and Rudolph, B. (1994): Die Börse als Marktplatz und Dienstleister, Marketing, Zeitschrift für Forschung und Praxis 16, 167-180.

Naik, N. Y., Neuberger, A., and Viswanathan, S. (1999): Trade Disclosure Regulation in Markets with Negotiated Trades, Review of Financial Studies 12, 873-900.

Naranjo, A., and Nimalendran, M. (2000): Government Intervention and Adverse Selection Costs in Foreign Exchange Markets, Review of Financial Studies 13, 453-477.

O'Hara, M. (1995): Market Microstructure Theory, Cambridge.

O'Hara, M. (2003): Presidential Address: Liquidity and Price Discovery, Journal of Finance 58, 1335-1354.

Pagano, M. (1989): Trading Volume and Asset Liquidity, Quarterly Journal of Economics 104, 255-274.

Picot, A., Bortenlänger, C., and Röhrl, H. (1996): Börsen im Wandel: Der Einfluss von Informationstechnologie und Wettbewerb auf die Organisation von Wertpapiermärkten, Fritz Knapp, Frankfurt am Main.

Rappoport, P. (2001): Comments on "Does Market Transparency Matter? A Case Study", in: Market Liquidity: Proceedings of a Workshop held at the BIS (Bank for International Settlement), BIS Papers No. 2, 143-144.

Sapp, Stephen G. (2002): Price Leadership in the Spot Foreign Exchange Market, Journal of Financial and Quantitative Analysis 37, 425-448.

Sarig, O. and Warga, A. (1989): Bond Price Data and Bond Market Liquidity, Journal of Financial and Quantitative Analysis 24, 367-378.

Schiereck, D. (1995): Internationale Börsenplatzentscheidungen institutioneller Investoren, Wiesbaden.

Schmidt, R. H. and Terberger, E. (1997): Grundzüge der Investitions- und Finanzierungstheorie, Wiesbaden

Schultz, P. (2001): Corporate Bond Trading Costs: A Peek Behind the Curtain, Journal of Finance 56, 677-698.

Seppi, D. (1990): Equilibrium Block Trading and Asymmetric Information, Journal of Finance 45, 73-94.

Shyy, G. and Lee, J.-H. (1995): Price Transmission and Information Asymmetry in Bund Futures Markets: LIFFE vs. DTB, Journal of Futures Markets 15, 87-99.

Stenzel, S. (1995): Außerbörslicher Aktienhandel – Umfang und Ursachen, Berlin.

Stock, J. H. and Watson, M. (1988): Testing for Common Trends, Journal of the American Statistical Association 83, 1097-1107.

Stoll, H. R. (1992): Principles of Trading Market Structure, Journal of Financial Services Research 6, 75-107.

Stucki, P. (2000): Ist der Telefonhandel für Obligationen am Ende?, Financial Markets and Portfolio Management 14, 333-338.

Subrahmanyam, A. (1997): Multi-Market Trading and the Informativeness of Stock Trades: An Empirical Intraday Analysis, Journal of Economics and Business 49, 515-531.

The Bond Market Association (2002): E-Commerce in the Fixed Income Markets - The 2002 Review of Electronic Transaction Systems, Washington.

The Bond Market Association (2005a): European Bond Pricing Sources and Services: Implications for Price Transparency in the European Bond Market.

The Bond Market Association (2005b): Research Quarterly, May 2005.

Theissen, E. (2002): Floor versus Screen Trading: Evidence from the German Stock Market, Journal of Institutional and Theoretical Economics 158, 32-54.

Tinic, S. M. and West, R. R. (1973): Competition and the Pricing of Dealer Service in the Over-the-Counter Stock Market, Journal of Financial and Quantitative Analysis 7, 1707-1727.

Tse, Y. and Zabotina, T. V. (2001): Transaction Costs and Market Quality: Open Outcry versus Electronic Trading, Journal of Futures Markets 21, 713-735.

Viswanathan, S. and Wang, J. (2002): Market Architecture: Limit-Order Book versus Dealership Markets, Journal of Financial Markets 5, 127-167.

Watson; Mark W. (1994): Vector Autoregressions and Cointegration, in: Engle, R., McFadden, D. (Eds.), Handbook of Econometrics, Vol. 4 North Holland, Amsterdam, 2843-2915.

White, H. (1980): A Heteroscedasticity-Consistent Covariance Matrix Estimator and a Direct Test for Heteroscedasticity, Econometrica 48, 817-838.

Williamson, O. E. (1975): Markets and Hierarchies: Analysis and Antitrust Implications, New York.

Williamson, O. E. (1990): Die ökonomischen Institutionen des Kapitalismus, Unternehmen, Märkte, Kooperationen, Tübingen.

Williamson, O. E. (1991): Comparative Economic Organization: The Analysis of Discrete Structural Alternatives, Administrative Science Quarterly 36, 269-296.

FSC
www.fsc.org
MIX
Papier | Fördert
gute Waldnutzung
FSC® C083411

Kolibri 360 GmbH
Ferdinand-Jühlke-Straße 7
99095 Erfurt, Deutschland
produktsicherheit@kolibri360.de